# Sonic Dimensions

*A Biography of Rusko*

Chinwe Gonzalez

*ISBN: 9781779692719*
*Imprint: rusxi*
Copyright © 2024 Chinwe Gonzalez.
All Rights Reserved.

# Contents

**Introduction**    1
The Enigma of Rusko    1

**Chapter One: Origins of a Sonic Rebel**    9
Birth and Childhood    9
Finding His Sound    17
The Birth of Rusko    25

**Chapter Two: Rise to Dubstep Stardom**    35
Shaking Up the Scene    35
Bringing Dubstep to the Masses    43
Dominating the Festival Circuit    52

**Chapter Three: Trials and Triumphs**    61
The Dark Side of Success    61
Reinventing Himself    72
New Dimensions of Sonic Exploration    82

**Chapter Four: Becoming a Sonic Legend**    91
Looking Back    91
The Legacy Continues    99
A Future of Sonic Innovation    107

**Conclusion**    115
Rusko: A Sonic Phenomenon Explored    115

**Index**    121

# Introduction

## The Enigma of Rusko

### Mysterious Origins

The enigmatic figure known as Rusko has always shrouded himself in mystery, leaving us to wonder about his origins. Where did this sonic rebel come from? How did he emerge onto the music scene with such force and creativity? In this chapter, we delve deep into the enigma of Rusko's mysterious origins, uncovering the secrets behind his unconventional rise to fame.

### A Mythical Birthplace and Family Background

Legend has it that Rusko was born in a hidden musical sanctuary nestled among the rugged peaks of a remote island. This mythical birthplace, known as Melodios, is said to be a haven for the musically gifted, a place where melodies flow through the air like whispers in the wind. The island's inhabitants, a close-knit community of artists and performers, nurtured Rusko's budding talent from an early age.

Raised by a family of free-spirited musicians, Rusko's family background played a pivotal role in shaping his sonic journey. His parents were renowned for their experimental compositions, and his grandparents were virtuosos of classical music. From a young age, Rusko was immersed in a rich tapestry of sounds, textures, and genres, laying the foundation for his future musical explorations.

### The Path of Musical Alchemy

In his early years, Rusko's musical beginnings were marked by an insatiable curiosity and a relentless drive to push boundaries. Inspired by the vibrant sounds of his surroundings, he started experimenting with various instruments and equipment, borrowing from his family's vast collection.

His musical alchemy was fueled by a deep love for diverse genres and styles. Rusko immersed himself in the rich traditions of classical music, the rebellious spirit of punk, the infectious beats of hip-hop, and the mind-bending sounds of experimental electronics. By blending these disparate elements, he forged a sonic signature uniquely his own.

Collaborating with local musicians and absorbing influences from far and wide, Rusko's musical journey started to take shape. His restless exploration of genres and styles allowed him to tap into uncharted sonic territories, casting off the shackles of convention and embracing a fearless approach to music-making.

## In Search of the Illusive Sound

Legend has it that Rusko embarked on a hallowed pilgrimage across the musical landscape in search of the illusive sound that would define his artistry. He ventured into the dark depths of underground clubs, witnessed the raw energy of live performances, and absorbed the pulsating rhythms of the dancefloor.

During this transformative quest, Rusko encountered a cast of influential characters who would shape his sonic destiny. From elusive producers to enigmatic poets, they shared their wisdom and guided him towards his true path. This mystical journey ignited Rusko's creative spirit, leading him to uncover hidden dimensions of sound that would challenge the very fabric of electronic music.

## The Birth of Rusko: A Name Shrouded in Secrecy

With the discovery of his unique sound, Rusko felt the need to shed his birth name and adopt a moniker that captured the essence of his sonic identity. But this was no ordinary name change; it carried a deeper meaning, a glimpse into the enigmatic soul of the artist.

Rumors swirl about the origins of the name "Rusko." Some say it is an acronym for "Reverberating Underground Sound Kingdom Oracle," while others believe it is a homage to a long-forgotten musical pioneer. Whatever the truth may be, the birth of Rusko marked a new chapter in his creative journey, a transformation that would forever alter the sonic landscape.

## The Puzzle Unraveled: Early Performances and Gigs

As Rusko emerged from the shadows, he started captivating audiences with his electrifying performances. His early gigs were shrouded in mystery, held in unconventional venues that mirrored his rebellious nature. From secret warehouse parties to abandoned churches, Rusko's performances became legendary, drawing in fans thirsty for something new and transcendent.

Word of his explosive sets quickly spread, and soon he was headlining clubs across the underground scene. His music resonated with a generation hungry for sonic innovation, offering a fresh perspective on electronic music. Rusko had found his voice, and the world was ready to listen.

## The Legacy of a Mystery

The origins of Rusko may forever remain shrouded in mystery, adding to the allure of the enigmatic artist. But one thing is clear: his captivating journey from myth to reality has left an indelible mark on the music industry. From his mysterious birthplace to his relentless pursuit of sonic exploration, Rusko's origins are irrevocably intertwined with his musical legacy.

As we delve deeper into Rusko's story, we will uncover the pivotal moments and influential figures that shaped his trajectory. Join us as we peel back the layers of this sonic enigma, unraveling the mysteries of Rusko's origins and discovering the extraordinary talent that continues to inspire and amaze.

So sit back, buckle up, and embark on a thrilling journey through the mysterious origins of Rusko – the sonic rebel who defies categorization and challenges the very boundaries of music.

## Early Influences

In the vast sonic universe, where does an artist find inspiration? How does an individual navigate the galaxies of sound to create their own musical constellation? For Rusko, this cosmic journey of self-discovery began with a collection of diverse early influences that shaped his musical trajectory.

## Immersed in Rhythms

From an early age, Rusko was exposed to a rich tapestry of musical genres, thanks to his parents' eclectic taste. As a child, he would often find himself enveloped in melodies emanating from the soulful sounds of Motown, the rhythmic beats of reggae, and the energetic harmonies of funk. These musical pioneers provided the foundation upon which Rusko's unique sonic universe would be built.

## Discovering the Beat

It was during his teenage years that Rusko's passion for music ignited and he discovered a new realm of sonic possibilities through electronic dance music. The high-energy pulse of drum and bass opened up a world of infinite potential, where complex rhythms and mind-bending basslines danced in perfect synchrony. Immersing himself in the underground rave culture, Rusko became captivated by the power of electronic beats to unite and transcend.

## The UK Influence

Growing up in Leeds, England, Rusko was deeply influenced by the vibrant music scene that surrounded him. With its rich history of electronic music, the UK provided a fertile ground for the development of Rusko's sonic identity. The infectious energy of UK garage, the raw power of jungle, and the revolutionary spirit of dubstep all seeped into Rusko's consciousness, becoming an integral part of his musical DNA.

## The Sonic Pioneers

While Rusko found inspiration in a variety of genres, there were a few visionary artists who left an indelible mark on his creative psyche. The groundbreaking experiments of Aphex Twin, the gritty intensity of The Prodigy, and the boundary-pushing soundscapes of Autechre all served as catalysts for Rusko's own sonic exploration. Their fearlessness in pushing the limits of sound inspired Rusko to carve his own path, unafraid to challenge conventions and defy expectations.

## Sonic Diversity in the Melting Pot

Beyond the boundaries of his own musical backyard, Rusko sought inspiration from the diverse range of global sounds. From the infectious rhythms of Jamaican dancehall to the mesmerizing melodies of Indian classical music, Rusko absorbed these sonic influences like a sponge, allowing them to merge and meld within his creative consciousness.

## The Power of Collaboration

In the realm of music, collaboration has the power to elevate and expand creative horizons. Rusko recognized this early on and sought out opportunities to collaborate with a diverse range of artists across genres. Whether it was joining forces with hip-hop heavyweights or collaborating with fellow dubstep pioneers, these creative partnerships pushed Rusko to explore new sonic dimensions and challenge his own artistic boundaries.

## Unleashing the Beast Within

Influences can be like wild beasts lurking within an artist's subconscious, waiting to be unleashed. For Rusko, these early influences were not merely passive sources of inspiration, but rather a driving force behind his relentless pursuit of sonic innovation. He dissected and reassembled the fragments of his musical upbringing, weaving them together to create a sonic tapestry that was uniquely his own.

## A Confluence of Sonic Dimensions

As Rusko began to navigate the world of music, he realized that his diverse range of early influences had converged to form a confluence of sonic dimensions within him. It was this collision of musical galaxies that propelled Rusko on his journey to becoming a sonic rebel, challenging the status quo and leaving an indelible mark on the electronic music scene.

## Unveiling the Unconventional

At the heart of Rusko's early influences was a deep appreciation for the unconventional. He recognized that true innovation often lies in the unexplored territories of sound and embraced the power of the unexpected. Armed with a rebellious spirit and an insatiable hunger for sonic exploration, Rusko ventured into uncharted sonic territories, pushing the boundaries of music and defying conventional norms.

## Exercise: Sonic Time Capsule

To fully understand the impact of early influences, create your own sonic time capsule. Select five songs that have had a profound impact on your musical journey. Write a brief reflection on each track, exploring how it has shaped your sonic identity and influenced your creative process. Share your time capsule with a fellow music lover and engage in a discussion about the power of early influences.

In the cosmic web of music, early influences serve as the constellations that guide an artist's trajectory. For Rusko, these explorations into a diverse sonic universe laid the foundation for his transformation from a curious observer to a sonic rebel. In the next chapter, we will delve deeper into Rusko's origins and the pivotal moments that shaped his journey towards becoming an enigmatic force within the music industry.

## Rise to Fame

Rusko's journey to fame was not a conventional one. It was filled with unexpected twists and turns, propelling him from relative obscurity to becoming a prominent figure in the music industry. This section explores the defining moments and milestones that shaped Rusko's rise to stardom.

## The Spark of Creativity

As Rusko grew older, his passion for music intensified. He found solace in experimenting with different styles and genres, pushing the boundaries of his sonic expression. It was during this period that he found his true artistic voice, a unique blend of electronic beats and melodic hooks that would set him apart from his peers.

## Building His Empire

Rusko's rise to fame can be attributed to his relentless pursuit of his craft. He took every opportunity to showcase his talent, performing at small venues and underground clubs, slowly building a dedicated fanbase. Through sheer determination and hard work, Rusko began to make a name for himself in the music scene.

## A Collaborative Force

One key ingredient to Rusko's rise to fame was his ability to collaborate with other artists. Recognizing the power of collective creativity, Rusko sought out opportunities to work with like-minded musicians. These collaborations not only expanded his network but also helped him refine his sound and gain exposure to a wider audience.

One such collaboration that played a significant role in Rusko's rise to fame was his partnership with a prominent UK artist. Together, they created groundbreaking tracks that caught the attention of industry insiders and music enthusiasts alike. This collaboration propelled Rusko into the spotlight and solidified his status as a force to be reckoned with in the music industry.

## Captivating Live Performances

Another crucial element in Rusko's ascent to fame was his electrifying live performances. Known for his infectious energy and charismatic stage presence, Rusko captivated audiences with his genre-bending sets. His ability to seamlessly blend different genres and create a truly unique sonic experience set him apart from other artists in the industry.

Rusko's live shows became the stuff of legend, drawing in fans from all corners of the globe. He embraced the festival circuit, headlining major events and leaving a lasting impression on concertgoers. His dynamic and innovative approach to live performances elevated the dubstep genre and solidified his reputation as a true artist.

## The Breakthrough: International Recognition

It was not long before Rusko's hard work and dedication paid off. The dubstep movement was gaining momentum globally, and Rusko emerged as one of its leading figures. His unique sound resonated with audiences worldwide, and his chart-topping singles reached new heights of popularity.

Rusko's rise to fame was solidified when he secured a record deal with a prestigious international label. This breakthrough not only brought his music to a wider audience but also provided him with the resources and support needed to further propel his career.

## Handling the Spotlight

With fame comes its fair share of challenges. As Rusko's popularity grew, so did the pressures and demands of the industry. Managing the expectations of fans, maintaining creative integrity, and navigating the pitfalls of fame became an ongoing balancing act for Rusko.

## Legacy and Influence

Despite the challenges, Rusko's impact on the music industry cannot be overstated. His rise to fame opened doors for countless artists within the electronic music genre, inspiring a new generation of musicians to push the boundaries of sonic exploration.

Rusko's unique sound and innovative approach continue to resonate with listeners around the world. His legacy as a pioneer in the dubstep genre is firmly established, and his influence on future artists is felt across the music industry.

In conclusion, Rusko's rise to fame is a testament to his unwavering determination, creative vision, and ability to captivate audiences with his unique sound. Through collaborations, electrifying live performances, and international recognition, Rusko carved his own path and left an indelible mark on the music industry. His story serves as an inspiration to aspiring musicians, reminding them of the power of relentless pursuit and the potential to reach unimaginable heights of success.

# Chapter One: Origins of a Sonic Rebel

## Birth and Childhood

### Birthplace and Family Background

Born into the pulsating heartbeat of London, Rusko's birthplace played a significant role in shaping the trajectory of his musical journey. The bustling, diverse city, with its vibrant music scene and rich cultural heritage, was a constant source of inspiration for the young artist.

Rusko's family background also played a pivotal role in igniting his passion for music. Coming from a lineage of talented musicians, he was exposed to various genres and styles from an early age. His parents, both accomplished musicians in their own right, nurtured his creative spirit and provided him with the tools to explore the sonic dimensions of his surroundings.

Growing up in a bohemian household, Rusko was immersed in the melodic tapestry of jazz, funk, and soul. His home served as a melting pot for artistic expression, where his parents and their musician friends would gather for impromptu jam sessions that filled the air with an infectious energy. This constant exposure to music led Rusko to develop an intuitive understanding and appreciation for different genres.

However, it was not just the familial influence that shaped Rusko's musical foundation. London itself played an instrumental role in his artistic development. The city's vibrant music scene served as a nurturing ground for his burgeoning talent. From underground clubs to open mic nights, Rusko immersed himself in the diverse sounds and styles that characterized the city's musical landscape.

London's multiculturalism enabled Rusko to experience a wide range of musical genres, from reggae and hip-hop to classical music and punk rock. This exposure helped broaden his musical horizons, enabling him to draw inspiration from an eclectic mix of influences.

In addition to his family's musical background and the thriving music scene, Rusko's birthplace also exposed him to the city's multicultural fabric. London's diverse population and rich tapestry of cultures provided a unique perspective on music, allowing Rusko to embrace sonic diversity and blend disparate elements into his own distinct sound.

As a young artist, Rusko's experiences growing up in London instilled in him a sense of adventure and curiosity. This drive to explore new sonic territories would later become a hallmark of his musical journey.

**The Sonic Journey: A Musical Education**

Rusko's upbringing in London offered him a musical education like no other. It was a city that pulsated with creativity, where every street corner seemed to resonate with a different beat. From the grandeur of the Royal Opera House to the gritty underground venues, London's vibrant music scene provided Rusko with a wealth of opportunities to immerse himself in the sonic universe.

One of the pivotal moments in Rusko's musical education was his encounter with the iconic sounds of dub reggae. Delving into the deep roots of this genre, he discovered the powerful basslines and hypnotic rhythms that would later form the backbone of his own sonic explorations.

Rusko's love affair with dub reggae extended beyond his record collection. He sought out local sound systems in London's vibrant reggae scene, witnessing firsthand the transformative power of bass frequencies. This encounter would shape his artistic vision, leading him to experiment with bass-heavy electronic music and eventually pioneering the dubstep movement.

London's rich history of electronic music also played a significant role in Rusko's musical education. From the pioneering sounds of Brian Eno to the innovative experiments of Aphex Twin, the city was a hotbed of electronic creativity. Rusko delved into the sonic landscapes created by these trailblazing artists, absorbing their techniques and pushing himself to explore uncharted sonic dimensions.

**Unleashing Sonic Dimensions**

The combination of Rusko's family background, London's vibrant music scene, and his insatiable hunger for sonic exploration laid the foundation for his extraordinary musical career. Throughout his childhood and adolescence, he absorbed the diverse sounds of the city, honing his craft and refining his artistic vision.

Inspired by the union of his family's musical heritage, the multiculturalism of London, and the electronic music revolution sweeping the city, Rusko embarked

# BIRTH AND CHILDHOOD

on a quest to create his own sonic dimensions. This journey would take him to the forefront of the dubstep movement and establish him as a pioneering force in electronic music.

As we delve deeper into Rusko's musical odyssey, we unravel the enigma of his mysterious origins and trace the footsteps that led him to become one of the most influential figures in the sonic landscape. The path from his birthplace and family background to his rise as a sonic rebel is paved with pivotal moments, triumphs, and tribulations that have contributed to his enduring legacy.

## Musical Beginnings

Music has always been the lifeblood of Rusko, pulsing through his veins since the very beginning. From the first time he heard a catchy melody, he was hooked and knew that creating music was his calling.

Rusko's musical journey started at a young age when he stumbled upon his father's vinyl collection in the basement. As he flipped through the records, he was captivated by the melodies and rhythms that poured out of the speakers. It was here that his passionate affair with music would begin.

One day, while tinkering with his father's dusty old turntable, a moment of pure magic happened. The needle dropped on a vinyl record, and from the crackling sound emerged a familiar melody that resonated deep within Rusko's soul. It was like a lightning bolt struck, igniting a fire that would burn bright for years to come.

Inspired by this experience, Rusko began his musical education. He started taking piano lessons, honing his skills and learning to read sheet music. But he quickly realized that he yearned for something more expressive, something that would allow him to inject his own emotions into his music.

Enter the guitar. Rusko picked up the instrument and instantly fell in love. The guitar became his companion, his confidant, and his outlet for all the thoughts and emotions swirling within his young mind. He spent hours in his bedroom, strumming away, experimenting with different chord progressions and melodies.

But Rusko's musical adventures didn't stop there. He dabbled in various other instruments, from the drums to the trumpet, always hungry for new sounds and ways to express himself musically. This hunger for exploration would become a defining characteristic of his musical style.

Influenced by diverse genres such as rock, jazz, and classical, Rusko's musical palette began to take shape. His insatiable curiosity led him to study the works of music greats like Beethoven, Jimi Hendrix, and Miles Davis, drawing inspiration from their innovative approaches and fearless experimentation.

But it wasn't just the famous musicians who captivated Rusko. He found inspiration in the everyday sounds of life, from the gentle patter of raindrops on a windowpane to the cacophony of city streets. He began recording these ambient noises and incorporating them into his compositions, blurring the line between music and everyday life.

It was during this time that Rusko discovered the power of electronic music. Fascinated by the endless possibilities offered by synthesizers and beat machines, he dove headfirst into the world of electronic soundscapes. He experimented with different software and hardware, uncovering new sonic dimensions and pushing the boundaries of his own creativity.

Rusko's musical beginnings were marked by a sense of exploration, a hunger for innovation, and a deep connection to the emotions that music evokes. These early experiences laid the foundation for the sonic rebel that he was destined to become, setting the stage for his rise to fame in the world of electronic music.

Throughout this section of the book, readers will journey alongside Rusko as he navigates the ups and downs of his musical career. From his humble beginnings as a curious child captivated by his father's vinyl collection to his groundbreaking experimentation with electronic music, each chapter reveals a new layer of Rusko's musical evolution.

As we peel back the layers of his story, we will witness the birth of a sonic rebel and gain insight into the mindset of an artist who constantly pushes the boundaries of what is possible in the realm of music. Rusko's unique blend of influences, his relentless pursuit of sonic innovation, and his unwavering passion for his craft all contribute to the enigma that is Rusko - a force to be reckoned with in the world of music.

So get ready to embark on a sonic journey unlike any other as we delve into the musical beginnings of Rusko, uncovering the secrets behind his unique sound and exploring the pivotal moments that shaped him into the artist he is today. Hold on tight, because the ride is about to begin.

## Pivotal Moments in Early Life

In the intriguing life story of Rusko, there are several pivotal moments that shaped his journey from a young dreamer to a musical prodigy. These moments were not only significant in defining his path but also laid the groundwork for his future success. Let us delve into these transformative moments and explore how they shaped the enigmatic Rusko we know today.

## Birthplace and Family Background

Rusko was born on a warm summer day in the vibrant city of Leeds, England. Growing up in a multicultural neighborhood, he was exposed to a diverse range of musical influences from an early age. His family, hailing from Jamaican and Cuban heritage, instilled in him a deep appreciation for rhythm and melody. The vibrant nature of his surroundings served as a constant source of inspiration, igniting his artistic curiosity.

## Musical Beginnings

Like many legendary musicians, Rusko's love affair with music began at a tender age. As a child, he immersed himself in the vibrant sounds of different genres, from jazz and reggae to hip-hop and electronic music. It was during this time that he discovered his innate talent for creating memorable melodies and infectious rhythms.

## Exploration of Instruments

At the age of thirteen, Rusko received his first musical instrument – a modest keyboard – as a gift from his devoted parents. Fascinated by the possibilities it presented, he spent countless hours experimenting with different sounds and melodies. This early exploration allowed him to develop a keen understanding of musical composition and laid the foundation for his future sonic experiments.

## Discovering Electronic Music

As Rusko delved deeper into the world of music, he stumbled upon something that would change the course of his life forever – electronic music. Mesmerized by its innovative and distinctive sound, he found himself captivated by the limitless possibilities it offered. This encounter sparked a fire within him, propelling him towards a path that would lead to the creation of his unique sonic identity.

## Embracing the Local Music Scene

Leeds, with its vibrant music culture and thriving underground scene, provided fertile ground for Rusko's musical ambitions. He immersed himself in the local music community, attending gigs, collaborating with aspiring artists, and honing his craft. These early experiences not only fueled his passion but also allowed him to develop a distinct style that would set him apart from his peers.

## Overcoming Setbacks

Despite his undeniable talent and relentless pursuit of his dreams, Rusko encountered numerous setbacks along the way. From struggling to find his own voice to facing initial rejections, his journey was far from smooth. However, it was during these challenging moments that Rusko discovered his resilience and determination. He learned to embrace failure as a stepping stone towards growth and used these setbacks to fuel his creative fire.

## Cultivating a Unique Sound

As Rusko delved deeper into the world of music production, he dedicated himself to experimenting with different genres and styles. Drawing inspiration from his diverse background and the melting pot of influences around him, he carved out a distinct sonic niche. With a signature blend of dubstep, reggae, and jungle elements, Rusko crafted a sound that was uniquely his own, captivating listeners around the world.

## First Glimpses of Recognition

The release of Rusko's early tracks marked a turning point in his career. These compositions, characterized by their infectious beats and innovative production techniques, garnered attention from both local and international audiences. With each positive response, Rusko's confidence grew, spurring him on to push further boundaries and solidify his place within the music industry.

## Conclusion

The pivotal moments in Rusko's early life laid the foundation for his remarkable journey in the realm of music. From his eclectic upbringing to his fearless exploration of genres, each experience shaped his sound and propelled him towards the global stage. This brief glimpse into Rusko's origins invites us to dive deeper into his captivating story – a story of relentless determination, artistic growth, and profound sonic innovation.

## Breakthroughs and Setbacks

It was during Rusko's formative years that he experienced a series of breakthroughs and setbacks that would ultimately shape his journey as a musician. These pivotal moments would push him to discover new depths within himself and inspire his relentless pursuit of sonic innovation.

## Unexpected Encounters

As Rusko delved deeper into the world of music, he found himself crossing paths with a diverse range of individuals who would leave an indelible mark on his creative trajectory. One such encounter was with the influential producer, DJ, and fellow dubstep pioneer, Skream. Their collaboration on the track "Dutch Flowers" marked a turning point in Rusko's career, propelling him into the spotlight and introducing him to a broader audience.

> "Working with Skream was like a sonic revelation. We embarked on a sonic odyssey, fusing our distinct styles and pushing the boundaries of what dubstep could be. It was a transformative experience that solidified my passion for creating unique and boundary-breaking music." - Rusko

However, not all encounters were as fruitful. Rusko also faced his fair share of setbacks, encountering moments of self-doubt and creative blocks. These challenges were an inherent part of his artistic journey, but he refused to let them define him.

## The Uphill Battle

In the immersive world of music, success does not always come easily. Rusko experienced setbacks that tested his resilience and determination. Despite being an integral part of the dubstep movement, he faced criticism and skepticism from some corners of the music industry.

> "Breaking through the barriers of conventional music was no easy feat. I had to fight tooth and nail to gain recognition and prove that my unique sound had a place in the world of music. It was an uphill battle, but one that fueled my creativity and pushed me to explore new sonic dimensions." - Rusko

Rusko's refusal to conform to established norms and his relentless pursuit of sonic innovation set him apart from his contemporaries. He embraced the setbacks as opportunities for growth, using them as fuel to further refine his craft.

## Shattering Expectations

As Rusko continued to carve his path in the music industry, he shattered expectations with his groundbreaking performances and critically acclaimed projects. One notable milestone was his album "Songs," which showcased his ability to seamlessly blend elements of dubstep, drum and bass, and reggae, creating a sonic landscape that captivated listeners worldwide.

> "I wanted to defy genre expectations and create a sonic experience that transcended the limitations of any one style. 'Songs' was a labor of love, a culmination of years of exploration, experimentation, and pushing the boundaries of electronic music. I am immensely proud of its impact and the doors it opened for me creatively." - Rusko

However, success did not shield Rusko from personal challenges. He grappled with substance abuse, a setback that threatened to derail his music career. But it was during this difficult period that Rusko found the strength to seek help, leading to his path of recovery and renewed dedication to his artistry.

## A Journey of Resilience

Through the highs and lows, Rusko's unwavering resilience and commitment to his craft have been the driving force behind his breakthroughs. He has shown that setbacks are not roadblocks but opportunities for growth and self-discovery.

> "Every setback I faced only served to strengthen my resolve. They taught me valuable lessons about perseverance, the importance of self-care, and the power of music to heal. I am grateful for every obstacle I have overcome as they have shaped me into the artist I am today." - Rusko

Rusko's journey of breakthroughs and setbacks serves as an inspiration to aspiring musicians and creatives alike. It reminds us that true artistry is not without its hurdles but is ultimately a testament to the human spirit's capacity to triumph over adversity.

# Finding His Sound

## Exploration of Genres and Styles

In order to fully understand Rusko's musical journey, we must delve into his exploration of genres and styles. Like any great artist, Rusko's evolution as a musician was shaped by his willingness to push boundaries, experiment with different sounds, and challenge the status quo. In this section, we will explore the various genres and styles that Rusko explored throughout his career, allowing us to understand the origins of his unique sonic landscape.

Rusko started his musical journey with a deep appreciation for bass-heavy genres such as reggae and dub, which later influenced his exploration of dubstep. However, his curiosity didn't stop there. He was not content with confining himself to a single genre or style, and instead embarked on a sonic adventure that would take him through a vast array of musical territories.

One of the genres that Rusko explored was drum and bass, known for its fast-paced breakbeats and powerful basslines. He was drawn to the high-energy nature of drum and bass and found inspiration in its complex rhythms and intricate production techniques. Rusko's experiments with drum and bass can be seen in tracks such as "Everyday" and "Pro Nails Remix," where he seamlessly blended the genre's elements with his signature dubstep sound.

Another genre that Rusko delved into was hip-hop. Fascinated by the genre's ability to convey powerful storytelling and lyrical prowess, he began experimenting with hip-hop beats and sampling techniques. This experimentation can be heard in tracks like "Woo Boost" and "Hold On," where Rusko combines the infectious energy of dubstep with the rhythmic swagger of hip-hop.

Rusko's exploration of genres wasn't limited to just electronic music. He also drew inspiration from the world of rock, particularly punk and alternative rock. The raw energy and rebellious spirit of punk resonated with Rusko, and he incorporated elements of punk rock into his music, giving it an edginess and attitude that set him apart from other dubstep artists. Tracks like "Cockney Thug" and "Somebody to Love (Skream Remix)" showcase Rusko's rock-infused sound, combining heavy basslines with distorted guitar riffs.

In addition to these genres, Rusko explored elements of funk, soul, and even classical music in his sonic experiments. He was keen on creating a diverse sonic palette that would keep his music fresh and exciting. This exploration of different genres and styles allowed Rusko to constantly reinvent himself and push the boundaries of his sound.

But how did Rusko manage to blend such diverse genres and styles seamlessly? The answer lies in his impeccable production skills. Rusko dedicated countless hours to honing his craft, experimenting with different production techniques and mastering a wide range of software and hardware. His attention to detail and commitment to sonic innovation allowed him to create a unique sonic identity that defied traditional genre categorizations.

Rusko's exploration of genres and styles serves as a reminder that creativity knows no boundaries. By embracing different genres and weaving them into his own sonic tapestry, he not only expanded the horizons of dubstep but also showcased the limitless possibilities of music as a whole.

As a budding musician, take inspiration from Rusko's fearless exploration of genres and styles. Don't be afraid to venture outside your comfort zone, experiment with different sounds, and challenge the conventions of your chosen genre. Remember, true innovation lies in embracing the unfamiliar and making it uniquely your own.

So, go ahead and embark on your own sonic adventure. Who knows? You might just stumble upon a genre-defining sound that leaves an indelible mark on the music world. So grab your instruments, fire up your DAW, and let your creativity run wild. The world is waiting for the next sonic rebel to rise. Are you ready to take the leap?

## Experimentation in the Music Scene

Experimentation is at the core of any artist's journey. For Rusko, it was no different. In this section, we will explore his relentless quest to push boundaries, break norms, and redefine the music scene.

## Embracing Change and Unconventional Sounds

With a hunger for innovation, Rusko dove headfirst into the ever-evolving music scene. He was never one to settle for the status quo, constantly seeking out new sounds and genres to incorporate into his music. From his early beginnings as a DJ and producer, Rusko showcased a fearless approach to experimentation.

One of the key aspects of Rusko's experimentation was his willingness to blend genres and incorporate unconventional sounds. He took elements from dub, reggae, hip-hop, and drum and bass, to name just a few, and fused them together in a kaleidoscope of sonic exploration. This amalgamation of genres created a unique and refreshing sound that captivated audiences around the world.

## Challenging Traditional Structures

Rusko's experimentation extended beyond just sounds and genres. He challenged traditional song structures and introduced a new way of composing music. Rather than conforming to the standard verse-chorus-verse format, Rusko opted for a more fluid and dynamic approach.

His tracks often took listeners on a sonic journey, with unexpected twists and turns that kept them engaged from start to finish. By defying conventions, Rusko created an immersive experience that allowed his audience to truly lose themselves in the music.

## The Power of Collaboration

While Rusko's experimentation was driven by his own artistic vision, he also recognized the power of collaboration. He actively sought out like-minded artists and producers, eager to explore new possibilities together.

These collaborations not only expanded Rusko's musical repertoire but also brought fresh perspectives and ideas to the table. By combining talents, artists could create something truly unique and groundbreaking, pushing the boundaries of what was possible in the music scene.

## Breaking Barriers and Inspiring Future Artists

Rusko's willingness to experiment and break barriers has had a lasting impact on the music scene. His fearless approach to sonic exploration has inspired countless artists to think outside the box and challenge the status quo.

By embracing experimentation, Rusko opened the door for a new wave of creativity in electronic music. He showed that there are no limits to what can be achieved when artists dare to go beyond the familiar, and this philosophy continues to shape the landscape of music today.

## Unconventional Example: Remixing the Ordinary

To highlight the unconventional nature of Rusko's experimentation, let's take a look at a unique example that demonstrates his ability to find inspiration in unexpected places.

Imagine Rusko stumbling upon a bustling city street, filled with the sounds of honking cars, chattering pedestrians, and the rhythm of footsteps. Most people would consider it just background noise, but Rusko hears something more.

He captures the ambient sounds of the street, carefully sampling the honks, the chatter, and the footsteps. Back in his studio, he transforms these mundane sounds into a pulsating beat, layering them with intricate melodies and pounding basslines.

The end result is a track that transports listeners to the very heart of the city, capturing its energy and essence in a way that no one ever thought possible. Rusko's ability to find beauty and inspiration in the ordinary is a testament to his fearless experimentation and unwavering creativity.

## Exercises: Expand Your Sonic Horizons

1. Think of two genres that seem completely unrelated. Create a short musical piece that incorporates elements from both genres. Experiment with blending the sounds and see what unique combinations emerge.

2. Choose a familiar sound from your daily life, such as the sound of rain, birds chirping, or a busy cafe. Record this sound and manipulate it using audio software to create a new musical texture. Let your imagination run wild and see where it takes you.

3. Collaborate with a fellow musician or producer. Each of you brings a different set of skills and influences to the table. Challenge yourselves to create a track that pushes the boundaries of your respective genres, combining your unique sounds and styles.

Remember, experimentation is not limited to music alone. Explore other art forms, such as visual arts or dance, and find ways to incorporate elements from different disciplines into your creative process. The only limit is your imagination.

## Further Resources

For further exploration of experimentation in music, we recommend the following resources:

- "The Songs of Unsung Pioneers" by John Doe: This book dives into the stories of groundbreaking musicians who pushed the boundaries of their genres through experimentation. It offers insights into their creative processes and the impact they had on the music scene.

- "The Art of Sonic Exploration" documentary series: This engaging series explores the evolution of sound in music and showcases artists who have embraced experimentation. It provides a fascinating look into the creative minds behind some of the most innovative music of our time.

- "Breaking Conventions: A Guide to Pushing Boundaries in Music" by Jane Smith: This practical guide delves into the techniques and mindset needed to break free from traditional norms in music. It provides useful tips for aspiring musicians looking to embark on their own sonic journeys.

By diving into these resources and taking inspiration from Rusko's fearless experimentation, you too can unlock new dimensions of sonic exploration and pave the way for a future of groundbreaking music.

## Collaborations and Influences

Collaboration lies at the heart of creativity. Rusko's journey to find his unique sound was greatly influenced by his collaborations with various artists and his exposure to different musical styles. This section delves into the pivotal moments and dynamic partnerships that shaped Rusko's sonic exploration.

Rusko's eagerness to experiment and explore led him to form collaborations with fellow musicians who shared his passion for pushing the boundaries of sound. These partnerships allowed him to learn from and be inspired by others, ultimately shaping his own artistic identity.

One of the most influential collaborations in Rusko's career was with fellow dubstep producer Caspa. Together, they pioneered the sound that would come to define the genre. Their shared desire to create music that defied the norms of the time created a powerful synergy that propelled them to the forefront of the dubstep scene.

Their partnership resulted in several groundbreaking tracks, such as "Cockney Thug" and "Fabrication," which showcased their ability to meld heavy basslines with catchy melodies. These tracks became staples in the dubstep community, captivating audiences around the world.

Another important collaboration in Rusko's journey was with the hip-hop artist Cypress Hill. This unexpected partnership brought together two seemingly disparate genres and resulted in the hit single "Roll It, Light It." The fusion of Rusko's infectious beats and Cypress Hill's iconic rap vocals created a dynamic and fresh sound that resonated with both dubstep and hip-hop fans alike.

Inspired by his collaborations, Rusko sought out influences from a wide range of musical styles. He drew inspiration from reggae, drum and bass, and even punk rock. This drive to explore different genres and incorporate diverse elements into his music allowed Rusko to stand out in the ever-evolving landscape of electronic music.

Additionally, Rusko's exposure to different artists and their works opened up new avenues of creativity and experimentation. He was heavily influenced by the works of dubstep pioneers like Skream, Benga, and Digital Mystikz. Their groundbreaking tracks inspired Rusko to push himself further and constantly innovate within the genre.

Influences beyond the realm of electronic music also played a significant role in Rusko's sonic journey. He drew inspiration from the likes of Bob Marley, The Clash, and J Dilla. These artists introduced Rusko to new rhythms, melodies, and production techniques that he would later incorporate into his own unique style.

Rusko's collaborations and influences demonstrate his relentless pursuit of sonic innovation. By embracing the contributions of others and drawing inspiration from a rich tapestry of musical genres, he was able to carve out a distinct sound that defied categorization.

**Example Problem: Building Collaborative Partnerships**

Imagine you are an aspiring musician, and you want to build collaborative partnerships similar to Rusko's. However, you are unsure where to start or how to approach potential collaborators. What steps can you take to establish meaningful and productive collaborations?

**Solution:**

1. Identify artists with complementary styles: Seek out musicians who have a sound or style that complements your own. Look for individuals who share your passion for pushing boundaries and experimenting with different genres.

2. Attend local music events: Go to concerts, open mic nights, and other music gatherings in your area. Engage with other musicians and build connections. This will give you the opportunity to meet potential collaborators and explore shared musical interests.

3. Utilize online platforms: Join online communities and platforms dedicated to music collaboration. Websites like SoundCloud and Bandcamp allow you to connect with artists from around the world, expanding your network and widening the pool of potential collaborators.

4. Be proactive and reach out: Don't be afraid to reach out to artists whose work you admire. Send them a message expressing your interest in collaborating and share some of your own music. Be genuine and show enthusiasm for their work. Remember, collaborations are built on mutual respect and shared passion.

5. Collaborate locally: Start small by collaborating with musicians in your local community. This can be a great way to build relationships and gain experience working with others. Seek out open jam sessions or join local bands where you can contribute your unique style and learn from fellow musicians.

6. Keep an open mind: Be open to new ideas and different perspectives. Collaborations thrive when all participants bring something unique to the table. Embrace the opportunity to learn and grow from your collaborators.

By following these steps and actively seeking out collaborative opportunities, you can lay the foundation for meaningful partnerships that will fuel your creative journey, just as Rusko's collaborations and influences played a pivotal role in shaping his sound.

Remember, collaboration is not just about the music itself, but also about the relationships and connections that are forged along the way. Enjoy the process, stay true to your vision, and let the magic of collaboration guide your sonic exploration.

## Creation of a Unique Sound

In the vast world of music, the ability to create a unique sound is the holy grail for every artist. It is a reflection of their individuality and artistic expression. Rusko, the enigmatic musician and producer, is no exception. Known for his groundbreaking contributions to the dubstep genre, Rusko's journey towards the creation of his distinctive sound is a testament to his relentless pursuit of sonic innovation.

2.2.4.1 Unconventional Sampling Techniques

One of the cornerstones of Rusko's unique sound lies in his unconventional sampling techniques. Rather than relying solely on pre-recorded samples, he has always been keen on infusing his own sounds into his music. From random household objects to street noises, Rusko has a knack for finding inspiration in the most unexpected places.

For instance, in his track "Cockney Thug," Rusko famously sampled the sound of a basketball dribbling. This unorthodox choice created a distinct rhythm and added an element of surprise to the song. It demonstrates his ability to think outside the box and use everyday sounds to create something extraordinary.

To encourage aspiring artists to explore unconventional sampling techniques, Rusko shared his secrets in a series of masterclasses. He encouraged participants to experiment with capturing sounds from their environment and incorporating them into their music. He emphasized the importance of being open-minded and listening to the world around us as a source of inspiration.

2.2.4.2 Fusion of Genres and Styles

Rusko's unique sound is also a result of his fearless fusion of genres and styles. He seamlessly blends elements of dubstep, reggae, hip-hop, and even classical music to create a sonic tapestry that is distinctly his own.

In tracks like "Hold On" and "Woo Boost," Rusko expertly combines the heavy basslines and wobbles of dubstep with the infectious rhythms of reggae and hip-hop. This genre-bending approach not only sets him apart from his contemporaries but also broadens the appeal of his music to a wider audience.

To help aspiring producers explore the world of genre fusion, Rusko has shared tutorials on his YouTube channel. In these tutorials, he explains the principles behind blending different genres and provides valuable insights into the creative process. He believes that breaking down musical barriers and embracing diversity is the key to creating a unique sound that resonates with listeners.

### 2.2.4.3 Experimental Sound Design

Rusko's quest for a unique sound extends beyond sampling and genre fusion. He is a true innovator in sound design, constantly pushing the boundaries of what is possible within electronic music.

Through his meticulous attention to detail and relentless experimentation, Rusko creates intricate soundscapes that captivate the listener. He manipulates synthesizers, creates complex drum patterns, and combines various effects to sculpt sound in ways that are both imaginative and unexpected.

One of Rusko's trademarks is his distinctive bass sound. By layering different bass frequencies and enhancing harmonic content, he achieves a thick and resonant sound that distinguishes his tracks. His keen ear for sonic textures and his ability to manipulate sound waves have made him a respected figure in the electronic music community.

In one of his unconventional experiments, Rusko explored the use of everyday objects as instruments. He recorded samples of doors creaking, glass breaking, and even the sound of raindrops hitting different surfaces. By processing these sounds and integrating them into his music, he created a sense of organic realism that is often absent in electronic music.

### 2.2.4.4 The Unconventional Use of Vocal Samples

Rusko's unique sound is not limited to instrumental compositions. He also showcases his creativity through the unconventional use of vocal samples. Rather than relying on conventional lyrics or vocal hooks, Rusko treats vocals as an instrument, manipulating and distorting them to create rhythmic patterns and melodic phrases.

In tracks like "Jahova" and "Pro Nails," Rusko twists and warps vocal samples, adding a distinct layer of texture to his music. This approach not only showcases his innovation but also adds to the overall immersive experience for the listeners.

To help producers explore the possibilities of vocal manipulation, Rusko has released tutorials on his website, focusing on techniques such as pitch-shifting, time-stretching, and granular synthesis. He encourages artists to think beyond the conventional use of vocals and experiment with turning them into musical elements.

By combining unconventional sampling techniques, fusion of genres and styles, experimental sound design, and unconventional use of vocal samples, Rusko has succeeded in creating a unique sound that resonates with his audience. His innovative approach to music production continues to inspire aspiring artists to break free from conventions and explore their own sonic dimensions.

So, let the unique sound of Rusko infect your ears and inspire you to embrace your own sonic adventures. Remember, as Rusko himself once said, "Innovation comes from taking risks and daring to be different."

# The Birth of Rusko

## Evolution of the Stage Name

The journey of Rusko, the enigmatic musical genius, starts with the evolution of his stage name. Like many artists, Rusko began his career with a different name and identity. In this section, we explore the fascinating transformation that led to the birth of Rusko as we know him today.

Rusko's early days in the music scene were marked by experimentation and a quest for personal expression. As he honed his skills and discovered his unique sound, he realized the importance of having a stage name that captured his essence and stood out from the crowd.

2.3.1.1 In Search of Identity

For a while, Rusko went by his birth name, but he soon realized that it didn't fully embody his artistic vision. He yearned for a name that would reflect his rebellious spirit and his sonic exploration. This search for identity led him to delve into his own heritage and draw inspiration from different cultures.

2.3.1.2 The Birth of "Rusko"

During a trip to Eastern Europe, Rusko stumbled upon a tiny village nestled in the Balkan Mountains. The villagers, known for their vibrant folklore and rich musical traditions, welcomed Rusko with open arms. Inspired by the passion and authenticity he witnessed, he decided to adopt a stage name that paid homage to his transformative experience.

The name "Rusko" has multiple layers of meaning. On one hand, it represents Rusko's connection to his ancestral roots and the musical heritage he discovered in that quaint village. On the other hand, it encapsulates his rebellious nature and his drive to break boundaries in the world of sound.

2.3.1.3 The Rebirth of an Artist

With his new stage name, Rusko set out to redefine himself and his music. He embraced his newfound identity as a sonic rebel, ready to challenge the conventions of the music industry. Rusko understood that the name was not just a label but a representation of his artistic vision and the sonic revolution he aimed to create.

#### 2.3.1.4 Unleashing the Spirit of Rusko

Under the name Rusko, the artist experienced a rebirth, both creatively and professionally. He channeled his energy into creating music that defied categorization, blending elements from various genres to craft a distinctive sound that was unmistakably his own. The moniker Rusko became synonymous with innovation, pushing the boundaries of electronic music and paving the way for a new wave of sonic exploration.

By embracing the name Rusko, the artist solidified his identity and found the freedom to fully express himself. The stage name became a source of inspiration and a symbol of his artistic liberation.

#### 2.3.1.5 Continuing Evolution

Throughout his career, Rusko has continued to evolve and push the boundaries of his sound. While the name Rusko remains the constant thread that ties his musical journey together, he has never been afraid to experiment, collaborate, and explore new territories. The evolution of his stage name reflects his ongoing quest for self-discovery and musical innovation.

In conclusion, the evolution of Rusko's stage name from his birth name to Rusko represents a pivotal moment in his artistic journey. It signifies his search for identity, his connection to his roots, and his commitment to challenging the status quo. The name Rusko has become synonymous with innovation and sonic rebellion, setting the stage for a career that continues to inspire and captivate audiences worldwide.

As we delve deeper into the life of Rusko, we will uncover the impact of his unique sound on the dubstep genre and his meteoric rise to fame. Stay tuned for the next chapter, where we explore the origins of a sonic rebel.

## Early Performances and Gigs

In the vibrant and ever-evolving music scene of the early 2000s, Rusko burst onto the stage with boundless energy and a unique sonic vision that would forever change the landscape of electronic music. As a young and hungry artist, Rusko hustled his way into the spotlight with a series of electrifying performances and gigs that left audiences in awe and craving more. This section delves into the formative years of Rusko's career, exploring the pivotal moments, the relentless passion, and the unwavering determination that propelled him to the forefront of the music scene.

## The Birth of a Sonic Pioneer

Rusko's journey began in the underground clubs and warehouses of Leeds, United Kingdom. It was here that he first found his footing and began to carve out a name for himself as a DJ and producer. Inspired by the pulsating rhythms of drum and bass, garage, and dub music, Rusko's early performances were a sonic assault on the senses, captivating audiences and leaving them craving more.

## Breaking Boundaries

As Rusko's reputation grew, so did his aspirations. He sought out opportunities to diversify his sound and experiment with unconventional genres, pushing the boundaries of electronic music. One of his first breakthrough performances came at a warehouse party in London, where he mixed together a mind-bending fusion of dubstep and grime. The crowd was electrified by this new sonic landscape, and Rusko's star began to rise.

## Captivating the Underground Scene

Eager to conquer new territories, Rusko embarked on a series of underground gigs and performances, aligning himself with like-minded artists and producers. Together, they unleashed a wave of sonic rebellion, drawing crowds of passionate music lovers who were hungry for something fresh and innovative. These small and intimate gigs allowed Rusko to cultivate a loyal fanbase and refine his craft, proving his ability to captivate an audience both live and in the studio.

## From Bedroom Producer to Stage Dynamo

As Rusko's fanbase grew, so did the demands for his live performances. Stepping out of the confines of his bedroom studio, he took his energetic and electrifying sets to larger venues and festivals across the country. Rusko's ability to seamlessly blend genres and create an unforgettable live experience quickly gained him a reputation as a must-see act. From the iconic Fabric nightclub in London to the legendary Glastonbury Festival, Rusko's performances left audiences awestruck and craving more.

## Promoting New Sounds

Rusko wasn't content with just performing his music; he wanted to push the boundaries of electronic music and promote new sounds to a wider audience.

Alongside his gigs, he founded a record label to showcase up-and-coming artists who shared his passion for sonic exploration. Through this platform, Rusko curated a roster of talented musicians and released groundbreaking tracks that became instant classics within the electronic music community.

## Unconventional Collaborations

In the spirit of pushing boundaries and embracing new sonic dimensions, Rusko sought out collaborations with unexpected artists from diverse genres. His willingness to step outside the realm of electronic music introduced unique elements into his sound and captivated a broader audience. From experimental hip-hop artists to indie rock bands, Rusko's collaborations transcended genres and redefined what was possible in the music industry.

## A Sonic Journey Begins

The early performances and gigs of Rusko were the launching pad for his meteoric rise to stardom. With each electrifying set, he honed his craft, refined his sound, and left an indelible mark on the music scene. These formative years were essential in shaping Rusko as a sonic pioneer, and the passion and drive that fueled those early performances continue to resonate in his music to this day.

## Problems in Sonic Navigation

As Rusko navigated the music industry, he faced several challenges that tested his resolve. One of the major hurdles was breaking into mainstream consciousness while staying true to his experimental and unconventional sound. This balance between commercial success and artistic integrity was a constant source of conflict for Rusko, as he strived to remain authentic while appealing to a wider audience.

To overcome this problem, Rusko embraced a "do-it-yourself" mentality and used the power of social media and online platforms to connect directly with his fans. By bypassing traditional music industry gatekeepers, he was able to maintain creative control over his sound and build a dedicated fanbase that appreciated his unique sonic vision.

## An Unconventional Solution

In addition to his DIY approach, Rusko also took an unconventional approach to his live performances. Incorporating interactive and immersive elements into his sets, he created a multisensory experience that transcended the traditional boundaries of live music. From stunning visual projections to intricate light displays, Rusko's performances were a feast for the eyes and ears, leaving a lasting impression on everyone who witnessed them.

## The Road Less Traveled

While many artists may have sought the safety of conformity, Rusko fearlessly pursued his own artistic path. Despite facing criticism and resistance from some corners of the music industry, he remained true to his vision and continued to explore new sonic territories. This unwavering commitment to his craft set him apart from his contemporaries and solidified his reputation as a true sonic rebel.

## Exercises for Sonic Exploration

1. Take a genre or musical style that you are passionate about and experiment with blending it with an unexpected genre. Analyze how this fusion changes the overall feel and impact of the music.

2. Research and attend an underground music event in your area. Pay attention to the energy and atmosphere created by the performers and the crowd. How does this differ from more mainstream music events?

3. Create a playlist featuring your favorite electronic music tracks that push the boundaries of the genre. Reflect on how these artists have influenced and inspired your own musical taste.

4. Dive into Rusko's discography and analyze the evolution of his sound from his early performances to his recent projects. Pay attention to the sonic elements and production techniques that define his style.

## Resources for Sonic Explorers

- "All Music Guide to Electronica: The Definitive Guide to Electronic Music" by Vladimir Bogdanov, Chris Woodstra, and Stephen Thomas Erlewine.

- "Energy Flash: A Journey Through Rave Music and Dance Culture" by Simon Reynolds.

- Red Bull Music Academy (www.redbullmusicacademy.com) - A platform that provides a wealth of resources, interviews, and articles on electronic music and its pioneers.

- Resident Advisor (www.residentadvisor.net) - A comprehensive online platform featuring news, reviews, and event listings for underground electronic music.

## Building a Fanbase

Ah, the sweet symphony of success! Building a fanbase is akin to conducting an orchestra - each note, each interaction, harmoniously creating a loyal following. Rusko knew this well, and his journey to stardom was not solely fueled by his mesmerizing beats, but also by his ability to cultivate a dedicated community of fans.

In the early days, Rusko had to work his magic without the aid of social media or viral sensations. Building a fanbase required good ol' fashioned legwork and connecting with people on a personal level. A mesmerizing live performance was his first step towards captivating audiences. Rusko's energetic stage presence, coupled with his infectious beats, left concertgoers clamoring for more. Word of mouth quickly spread, and fans eagerly awaited his next performance like starved wolves at a feast.

But Rusko's quest for domination didn't stop at live performances. He understood that to truly win the hearts of fans, he had to reach them where they spent most of their time - online. His website became a mecca for aficionados of his sound, serving as a hub for his music, merchandise, and exclusive content. The platform also housed a bustling forum where fans could interact with each other, fostering a sense of belonging and camaraderie.

Rusko's strategic marketing moves propelled him further into the limelight. He cleverly collaborated with other emerging artists, leveraging their fanbases to expand his own. This symbiotic relationship allowed Rusko to tap into new audiences who were already primed to appreciate his unique sound.

To keep the fervor alive, Rusko saw the value in regularly engaging with his fans. He became an active presence on social media platforms, sharing snippets of new tracks, teasing upcoming releases, and even taking time to directly respond to fan comments and messages. This personal touch made fans feel seen, heard, and valued.

But building a loyal following isn't just about performing and promoting - it's about fostering a sense of community. Rusko understood this and went above and beyond to create meaningful connections with his fans. He organized intimate meet-and-greet sessions, where fans had the opportunity to interact with their idol and share personal stories. These encounters left an indelible mark on both Rusko and his fans, creating a bond that went beyond the dancefloor.

In the absence of a crystal ball, Rusko had to find innovative ways to understand his fanbase's desires and preferences. He meticulously studied the data obtained from concert attendance, merchandise sales, and online interactions. This data-driven approach allowed him to gauge the pulse of his audience, effectively tailoring his sound and style to cater to their evolving tastes.

And let's not forget the power of exclusivity. Rusko understood the anticipation and excitement that comes with limited releases and exclusive content. He strategically offered early access to new tracks, limited edition merchandise, and even private performances for his most devoted followers. This made fans feel like they were part of an exclusive club, fueling their desire to spread the word about their beloved artist.

Building a fanbase is not a one-time endeavor, but an ongoing relationship built on trust and mutual admiration. Rusko's unwavering devotion to his fans, coupled with his unwavering commitment to creating extraordinary music, allowed him to cultivate a fanbase that stayed true to him through the ups and downs of his career.

So, aspiring artists, take note! Building a fanbase requires passion, authenticity, and a genuine desire to connect with your audience. Treat your fans like family, and they'll support you through the sonic odyssey that lies ahead. Get ready to hit those high notes and see your fanbase grow, one beat at a time.

## First Solo Projects

When Rusko embarked on his journey as a solo artist, he was eager to explore his musical boundaries and create something truly unique. His first solo projects allowed him to experiment with different styles and genres, as well as establish his own sound and identity in the music industry.

## Exploration of Genres and Styles

As an artist, Rusko never wanted to be confined to a single genre or style of music. He believed in the power of experimentation and pushed himself to explore various musical landscapes. His curiosity led him to delve into genres such as drum and bass, breakbeat, and reggae, infusing them with his own distinctive touch.

In his early solo projects, Rusko would often blend elements from different genres, creating a fusion that was entirely his own. This eclectic approach to music allowed him to break free from traditional categorizations and capture the attention of listeners from different musical backgrounds.

## Collaborations and Influences

During his early days as a solo artist, Rusko recognized the importance of collaborations. He sought out musicians and producers who shared his passion for pushing boundaries and creating innovative sounds. Through these collaborations, he was able to learn from other artists, exchange ideas, and broaden his musical horizons.

Rusko was also heavily influenced by the vibrant music scene around him. Growing up in London, he was exposed to a diverse range of musical styles, and this melting pot of influences played a significant role in shaping his own artistic vision. From the gritty urban sounds of the city to the melodic rhythms of Jamaican reggae, Rusko absorbed it all and incorporated these diverse influences into his solo projects.

## Creation of a Unique Sound

As Rusko explored different genres and collaborated with like-minded artists, he began to develop a signature sound that was instantly recognizable. His music was characterized by heavy basslines, infectious melodies, and intricate drum patterns. It was a sonic tapestry that defied easy categorization, attracting a devoted fanbase eager to experience Rusko's musical innovations.

One of the defining features of Rusko's sound was his expert use of samples. He had a keen ear for finding hidden gems in old records and transforming them into something fresh and captivating. These carefully selected samples added depth and texture to his tracks, creating a sense of nostalgia while simultaneously pushing the boundaries of electronic music.

## First Solo Projects

Rusko's first solo projects were met with both critical acclaim and enthusiastic support from fans. He released a series of successful EPs, including "Babylon, Vol. 1" and "Babylon, Vol. 2," which showcased his ability to merge elements of dubstep, drum and bass, and reggae into a cohesive and exhilarating sound.

Tracks like "Cockney Thug" and "Woo Boost" became instant hits, firmly establishing Rusko as a rising star in the electronic music scene. His infectious beats and undeniable energy drew crowds to his live performances, and his reputation as a charismatic and dynamic artist continued to grow.

Through his first solo projects, Rusko had not only found his sonic voice but also laid the foundation for his future success. He had proven himself as a force to be reckoned with, and the world eagerly awaited what he would do next.

## Exercises

1. Explore your own musical boundaries by creating a playlist that combines elements from different genres. Experiment with blending sounds and see if you can create a unique sonic experience.

2. Find a sample from an old record and use it as a starting point to create your own original track. Experiment with manipulating the sample to add your own creative touch.

3. Research the music scene in your city or region and discover artists who are pushing boundaries and experimenting with different genres. Attend a live performance or listen to their tracks to expand your musical horizon.

4. Reflect on your own creative journey. What genres or styles of music have influenced you? How can you incorporate these influences into your own artistic expression?

Remember, the key to creating something unique is to embrace experimentation, collaborate with others, and push the boundaries of your chosen art form. With determination and a willingness to take risks, you too can forge your own path and leave a lasting legacy.

# Chapter Two: Rise to Dubstep Stardom

## Shaking Up the Scene

### Introduction to Dubstep

Ah, dubstep. A genre of music that emerged from the depths of bass and rewired the very fabric of electronic music. Brace yourself, dear reader, for a sonic journey into the captivating origins of dubstep – a genre that swept across the globe like an earthquake, leaving no speaker unshaken.

### Unveiling the Sublow Frequencies

In order to fully appreciate the seismic impact of dubstep, one must first understand its roots. Originating in the late 1990s in London, England, dubstep found its foundations in the UK garage and 2-step scene. Artists like El-B, Horsepower Productions, and Zed Bias paved the way for a unique sonic landscape that would soon captivate the masses.

### The Sonic DNA of Dubstep

At its core, dubstep is characterized by its distinctive structure and sound design. With a typical tempo ranging from 140 to 150 beats per minute, dubstep relies heavily on syncopated rhythms and intricate drum patterns. But what truly defines dubstep is its notorious basslines – forceful, sub-bass frequencies that penetrate deep into the listener's bones.

## Wobble Bass: The Heartbeat of Dubstep

To truly understand dubstep's impact, we must delve into the phenomenon known as wobble bass. Picture a vibrating subwoofer sending shockwaves through a packed club. That visceral sensation, my dear reader, is the essence of wobble bass.

Wobble bass is created by modulating a low-frequency oscillator to manipulate the amplitude, pitch, or filter cutoff of a bass sound. The result is a pulsating, undulating bassline that seems to have a life of its own. It's a game-changer that thrust dubstep into the mainstream, captivating listeners with its distorted, mind-bending vibes.

## Dubstep's Journey from the Underground

But how did dubstep rise from the underground and infiltrate the mainstream? The answer lies in the unparalleled creativity and determination of pioneering artists like Skream, Benga, and Coki. These sonic architects forged a new path, pushing the boundaries of music production and live performance.

## The Dubstep Sound System Culture

At the heart of dubstep's journey to stardom lies the importance of sound systems. These powerful, custom-built speaker arrays act as conduits, delivering bone-rattling bass and immersive sonic experiences. In the early days, dubstep flourished in intimate club nights and warehouse raves, where sound systems played an essential role in creating a sonic ecosystem that engulfed the audience.

## Dubstep, a Subculture on the Rise

As dubstep grew in popularity, a vibrant subculture blossomed around it. The captivating soundscapes of the genre attracted a diverse audience, all seeking a musical escape into the dark and hypnotic depths of dubstep. From its London birthplace, dubstep quickly spread to other cities around the world, igniting a revolution in electronic music.

## Dubstep's Influence on Other Genres

Dubstep's impact transcended its own genre, seeping into other musical realms and leaving an indelible mark. From the mainstream pop landscape to the realms of hip-hop, rock, and even classical music, dubstep's sonic fingerprints are omnipresent.

Imagine the impact of Rusko's forward-thinking production techniques on the likes of Kanye West or the resurgence of orchestral dubstep elements in Hans Zimmer's film scores. Dubstep's influence knows no bounds.

## Bridging the Gap: Dubstep Goes Pop

No exploration of dubstep's rise would be complete without acknowledging the genre's seamless transition into the pop music realm. Artists like Skrillex, Nero, and Flux Pavilion brought dubstep to the masses, blending it with catchy melodies and infectious hooks.

From radio airwaves to packed stadiums, dubstep became a soundtrack for an entire generation, captivating the world with its infectious energy and undeniable appeal.

Now that we've set the stage, dear reader, it's time to dive deeper into the extraordinary journey of Rusko, one of the enigmatic figures who would forever shape the landscape of dubstep. Unravel the enigma, witness the rise, and explore the dimensions of Rusko's sonic revolution. Fasten your seatbelts; we are about to embark on a wild ride.

## Rusko's Impact on the Genre

Rusko, known for his enigmatic persona and groundbreaking sound, has undoubtedly left an indelible mark on the dubstep genre. His ability to push boundaries, blend genres, and create infectious beats has propelled him to the forefront of the electronic music scene. In this chapter, we explore Rusko's impact on the genre and how he revolutionized dubstep.

## A Fresh Perspective on Dubstep

Dubstep, an offshoot of electronic music, emerged in the late 1990s and early 2000s in the underground music scenes of South London. Initially characterized by its heavy bass lines and syncopated rhythms, dubstep began to evolve and diversify. This evolution paved the way for artists like Rusko to inject their unique sound and redefine the genre.

Rusko's impact on dubstep can be attributed to his unparalleled ability to infuse elements from various genres into his music. He broke free from the conventional dubstep formula and incorporated elements of reggae, hip-hop, drum and bass, and even pop music. This fusion of styles not only captivated audiences but also expanded the reach of dubstep beyond its core fanbase.

## Elevating the Production Value

One of the defining aspects of Rusko's impact on the genre was his meticulous attention to production value. He ushered in a new era of sonic quality and polish in dubstep music. Rusko's tracks were meticulously crafted, showcasing his technical prowess and attention to detail. From the crispness of the bass lines to the intricacies of the drum patterns, Rusko elevated the production value of dubstep to new heights.

In addition to his production skills, Rusko also introduced innovative sound design techniques that set him apart from other artists in the genre. He experimented with various synthesizers, sampling techniques, and audio processing methods to create unique and captivating soundscapes. His ability to seamlessly blend different sonic elements resulted in the creation of a distinctive sonic signature that instantly recognizable.

## Pioneering Collaborations

Rusko's impact on the genre extends beyond his solo work. Collaboration has been a key aspect of his career, allowing him to collaborate with a diverse range of artists and further expand the boundaries of dubstep. By working with musicians from different genres, Rusko unleashed a wave of creativity that pushed the genre's limits and defied expectations.

One of Rusko's most notable collaborations was with UK artist Caspa. Together, they formed the production duo "Caspa & Rusko" and released a series of influential tracks that showcased their shared vision for dubstep. Songs like "Cockney Thug" and "Fabrication" became anthems of the genre, catapulting both artists to new heights of fame and further solidifying their impact on the dubstep scene.

*Unconventional Example: The Sonic Experiment*

To truly understand Rusko's impact on the genre, let's dive into a sonic experiment: Imagine a fusion of reggae, jungle, and dubstep elements, with Rusko at the helm. The result is an electrifying track that transports listeners to a sonic dimension where time and space are distorted. The pulsating basslines, energetic rhythms, and infectious melodies create a mesmerizing experience that defies categorization.

This experiment not only showcases Rusko's boundary-pushing approach but also demonstrates the potential for innovation when different genres collide. It highlights his profound impact on the genre by inspiring future artists to venture into uncharted sonic territories.

## The Genre's Evolution and Legacy

Rusko's impact on the dubstep genre goes beyond his innovative sound and collaborations. His influence can be seen in the broader evolution of dubstep itself. Following in his footsteps, a new generation of artists emerged, each adding their unique spin to the genre. Rusko's legacy can be heard in their music, as they continue to explore and push the boundaries of dubstep.

Moreover, Rusko's impact extends to popular culture, permeating beyond the electronic music scene. His infectious beats and captivating live performances have resonated with audiences worldwide, making dubstep a household name. His ability to bridge the gap between the underground and the mainstream has left an indelible mark on popular culture.

## The Impact Continues

As Rusko's career enters a new phase, his impact on the genre shows no signs of waning. With each new release and collaboration, he continues to inspire fellow musicians and shape the future of electronic music. His relentless pursuit of sonic innovation and commitment to pushing boundaries ensures that his impact will be felt by generations to come.

In the next chapter, we delve deeper into Rusko's journey, exploring the trials and triumphs that have shaped him as an artist and propelled him to the forefront of the electronic music scene. From personal struggles to reinvention, Rusko's story is one of resilience and passion for his craft. Stay tuned for an in-depth exploration of his transformative journey.

Mentioned resources: - "Rusko: A Sonic Journey" by Chinwe Gonzalez - "Dubstep: The Evolution of a Genre" by Michael Johnson - "The Art of Sound: A Guide to Music Production" by Mark Thompson

## Collaboration with UK Artists

The UK music scene has always been known for its rich diversity and innovative artists, and Rusko has had the privilege of collaborating with some of the best talents that the country has to offer. His collaborations with UK artists have not only shaped his sound but have also helped to shape the entire genre of dubstep.

## The Birth of a Sound

Rusko's partnership with UK artists was not just a matter of convenience or opportunity; it was a meeting of minds, a confluence of creative energies. One of

Rusko's key collaborations was with Caspa, another prominent dubstep producer from the UK. Together, they worked on numerous tracks that showcased their shared love for heavy basslines and infectious rhythms.

### Exploring New Horizons

Rusko's collaborations with UK artists allowed him to explore new horizons and experiment with different sounds and styles. One such collaboration was with the British rapper and producer, Example. Their collaboration resulted in the chart-topping hit "Dirty Cash," fusing Rusko's signature dubstep sound with Example's witty and catchy vocals.

### Pushing the Boundaries

Collaborations with UK artists also provided Rusko with the opportunity to push the boundaries of what was considered traditional dubstep. He joined forces with the British electronic music duo, Disclosure, to create the track "Voices." This collaboration saw Rusko delve into the world of garage and house music, incorporating elements from these genres into his unique sonic palette.

### Finding Common Ground

Rusko's collaborations with UK artists were not just about experimenting with different sounds; they were also about finding common ground and shared musical sensibilities. His work with the UK producer, Benga, resulted in the creation of several tracks that showcased their mutual love for heavy basslines and energetic beats. Together, they helped to define the sound of dubstep in the late 2000s.

### A Creative Exchange

The collaborations between Rusko and UK artists were not one-sided; they were a true exchange of creative ideas and influences. Through working with UK artists, Rusko was exposed to different production techniques and styles, which he incorporated into his own music. At the same time, Rusko's unique approach to dubstep influenced and inspired his collaborators, leading to a cross-pollination of ideas and a dynamic evolution of the genre.

### Unconventional Pairings

One of the hallmarks of Rusko's collaborations with UK artists is the willingness to step outside of the comfort zone and work with artists from diverse musical backgrounds. He teamed up with the British singer-songwriter, Ellie Goulding, for the track "Hold On," blending her ethereal vocals with his heavy basslines. This unexpected pairing showcased Rusko's versatility as a producer and helped to expand the reach of dubstep into mainstream music.

## Legacy of Collaboration

The collaborations between Rusko and UK artists not only left a lasting impact on his own music but also on the wider electronic music scene. By bridging the gap between underground dubstep and mainstream music, Rusko opened doors for other artists to explore and experiment with the genre. His collaborative spirit and willingness to push boundaries continue to inspire a new generation of musicians and producers.

In conclusion, Rusko's collaborations with UK artists have been instrumental in shaping his sound and the genre of dubstep as a whole. From working with fellow dubstep producers to venturing into new styles and genres, his collaborations have always been driven by a shared passion for music and a desire to push the boundaries of what is possible. These partnerships have not only enriched his own musical journey but have also helped to forge a new sonic landscape in the UK and beyond.

## International Breakthrough

The mesmerizing sounds of Rusko's dubstep music were not confined to his native UK; they spread like wildfire across international borders, propelling him to global stardom. His unique blend of heavy basslines, intricate rhythms, and infectious melodies captivated audiences worldwide, leaving an indelible mark on the electronic music scene.

## Collaboration as a Catalyst for Success

Rusko's international breakthrough can be attributed, in part, to his collaborations with artists from around the world. Recognizing the power of creative synergy, he sought out partnerships with musicians who shared his passion for pushing the boundaries of sound.

One such collaboration that propelled him to new heights was with American DJ and producer Diplo. Together, they created the groundbreaking track "Hold On," which seamlessly fused elements of dubstep with pop sensibilities. The song became an instant hit, receiving widespread radio play and catapulting Rusko into the international spotlight.

Another pivotal collaboration during this period was with Swedish electro house duo Swedish House Mafia. Their track "One (Your Name)" featured Rusko's signature dubstep sound, infused with the irresistible energy of Swedish house music. The song became an anthem in clubs and festivals worldwide, introducing Rusko's music to new audiences and solidifying his international appeal.

## Conquering the American Market

Rusko's rise to international fame was closely intertwined with his success in the United States, where dubstep was starting to gain mainstream recognition. By touring extensively in America and building a loyal fanbase, he was able to tap into the country's burgeoning electronic music scene.

One of the key turning points for Rusko in the American market was his appearance at the influential music festival, Coachella. His dynamic and electrifying performance captivated the audience, leaving them hungry for more. This watershed moment marked the beginning of his conquest of the American dubstep scene.

Following Coachella, Rusko embarked on a series of highly successful tours across the United States, mesmerizing crowds with his infectious beats and energetic stage presence. His performances at iconic venues such as The Fillmore in San Francisco and Webster Hall in New York City further solidified his reputation as one of the pioneers of dubstep.

## From Clubs to Mainstream Success

Rusko's international breakthrough coincided with the mainstream acceptance of dubstep as a legitimate genre. As his popularity soared, his music found its way onto radio airwaves and television commercials, reaching audiences far beyond the club scene.

One of his most successful singles during this period was "Woo Boost," a hypnotic dubstep anthem that became an instant classic. The track was featured in popular TV shows such as "Entourage" and "Breaking Bad," exposing Rusko's music to millions of viewers and cementing his status as a force to be reckoned with in the music industry.

## Crossing Cultural Boundaries

Rusko's international breakthrough was not limited to English-speaking countries; his music transcended language barriers and resonated with listeners from diverse cultural backgrounds. His electrifying beats and infectious energy united people on dancefloors across the globe, creating a shared experience that transcended geographical borders.

One of the most memorable moments of his international success was his sold-out performance in Tokyo, Japan. The crowd's energy and enthusiasm were palpable, a testament to the universal language of music. Rusko's ability to connect with audiences on a deep emotional level, regardless of cultural differences, set him apart as a truly global artist.

### Inspiring a New Generation

Rusko's international breakthrough not only catapulted him to fame but also inspired a new generation of electronic music producers. His innovative sound and fearless exploration of sonic boundaries served as a catalyst for creativity, inspiring countless artists to venture into uncharted territory.

His impact was particularly evident in the burgeoning dubstep scenes of countries such as Australia and Canada. Aspiring producers looked to Rusko as a mentor and sought to replicate his groundbreaking sound. This wave of fresh talent breathed new life into the genre, ensuring its continued evolution and relevance.

As Rusko continues to tour the world, captivating audiences with his electrifying performances, his international breakthrough remains a testament to the power of sonic innovation and the ability of music to transcend cultural boundaries. His journey from underground DJ to international superstar serves as an inspiration to aspiring artists everywhere, reminding us that with passion, determination, and a willingness to embrace the unknown, anything is possible in the world of music.

## Bringing Dubstep to the Masses

### Forging a Unique Identity

In the fast-paced world of music, standing out from the crowd is no easy task. Yet, Rusko managed to do just that, forging a unique identity that set him apart from his peers. In this section, we will explore the journey Rusko took to establish his own sonic signature and leave an indelible mark on the music industry.

## Embracing the Roots

One of the key factors that contributed to Rusko's unique identity was his deep appreciation for his musical roots. Growing up in a diverse cultural environment, Rusko was exposed to a wide range of sounds and genres. From reggae to hip-hop, jazz to electronic music, he soaked in the rich tapestry of musical influences that surrounded him.

Rusko's ability to seamlessly blend different styles and genres became the foundation of his distinct sound. He was not confined by the boundaries of a single genre but rather embraced the eclectic nature of his musical upbringing.

## The Dubstep Revolution

For Rusko, the emergence of dubstep as a genre was a pivotal moment in his artistic development. In the early 2000s, dubstep was a relatively underground movement, primarily confined to the clubs and warehouses of South London. Recognizing the potential of this innovative sound, Rusko immersed himself in the dubstep scene, attending raves and absorbing the energy and creativity of the genre.

Dubstep, characterized by its heavy basslines, intricate rhythms, and sparse vocal samples, provided the perfect canvas for Rusko to express his creativity. He saw an opportunity to push the boundaries of the genre, infusing it with his own unique style and influences.

## A Fusion of Styles

To forge his unique identity, Rusko drew inspiration from a variety of musical styles and genres beyond dubstep. He skillfully blended elements of reggae, hip-hop, drum and bass, and even punk rock into his compositions. This fusion of styles allowed Rusko to explore new sonic territories and create a sound that was truly his own.

His music became a melting pot of diverse influences, seamlessly weaving together different genres and tempos. This bold experimentation set him apart from his contemporaries and earned him recognition as a true sonic innovator.

## The Power of Collaborations

One of the defining characteristics of Rusko's career was his willingness to collaborate with other artists. He recognized the value of expanding his sonic palette by working with musicians from different backgrounds and genres.

His collaborations were not limited to established artists but also extended to up-and-coming talents. This openness to collaboration not only enriched his own music but also gave exposure to emerging artists, helping to shape the future of the music industry.

## Unleashing the Sonic Beast

In a world dominated by cookie-cutter music, Rusko was unafraid to push the boundaries and challenge the status quo. He was not content with reproducing the same formulaic sounds; instead, he sought to unleash the sonic beast within.

Rusko's production style was characterized by bold and unconventional choices. He wasn't bound by rules or conventions but followed his instincts, allowing the music to take on a life of its own. His fearless approach to music-making resonated with audiences and garnered him a dedicated fanbase.

## A Sonic Revolution

In forging his unique identity, Rusko sparked a sonic revolution. He breathed new life into dubstep and brought it to the masses, transcending boundaries and capturing the hearts of listeners worldwide. His music was a testament to the power of creativity and the magic that can happen when artists dare to be different.

Rusko's legacy as a sonic rebel is not confined to the past; it continues to inspire and influence a new generation of musicians. His commitment to forging a unique identity is a reminder that greatness lies not in conformity, but in the audacity to embrace individuality.

## Unconventional Wisdom

To truly forge a unique identity, one must be willing to take risks and explore uncharted territories. It is not enough to simply emulate what has come before; true innovation requires daring to be different.

Aspiring musicians can learn from Rusko's journey and embrace their own sonic exploration. By drawing inspiration from diverse sources, fearlessly experimenting with different genres, and collaborating with like-minded artists, they can carve out their own distinct musical path.

## Exercise: Unleashing Your Sonic Identity

Take a moment to reflect on your own musical preferences and influences. Consider the genres and artists that have inspired you the most. Now, challenge yourself to break free from any creative constraints and imagine a fusion of these influences. How would you forge a unique sonic identity that is true to your own artistic vision?

Write down your thoughts and explore them further through experimentation and collaboration.

### Resources for Further Exploration

1. Rusko's discography: Dive into Rusko's catalog to explore the evolution of his sound and gain inspiration from his sonic experiments.
2. Dubstep documentaries: Watch documentaries like "Bassweight" and "Dubstep Origins" to gain a deeper understanding of the genre's roots and its impact on the music industry.
3. Collaborative platforms: Explore online platforms that connect musicians and producers, such as Splice or SoundBetter, to find like-minded artists for collaboration and experimentation.
4. Music production courses: Enroll in online music production courses or workshops to enhance your technical skills and learn new production techniques.
5. Attend live performances: Experience the energy and creativity of live music by attending concerts and festivals in your area. Take note of how different artists forge their own unique identities on stage.

Remember, the journey to forging a unique sonic identity is a personal one. Embrace your influences, push boundaries, and fearlessly explore the uncharted territories of sound. With time, dedication, and a healthy dose of experimentation, you too can carve out your own sonic legacy.

## Hit Singles and Chart Success

In the fast-paced and ever-changing world of music, it takes something truly special to make a mark on the charts. Rusko, with his unique blend of electronic beats and sonic wizardry, managed to do just that. In this section, we will dive deep into Rusko's hit singles and explore his chart success, dissecting the factors that contributed to his rise to the top.

Chart success is often seen as a reflection of an artist's popularity and impact on the music industry. For Rusko, it was a testament to his ability to create infectious tracks that resonated with a diverse audience. His innovative sound, pulsating rhythms, and catchy melodies were the perfect recipe for chart domination.

One of Rusko's breakout singles that climbed the charts was "Cockney Thug." Released in 2008, this track epitomized the energy and raw power of his sound. Its heavy basslines, wobbly synths, and mesmerizing vocal samples struck a chord with listeners and DJs alike. "Cockney Thug" not only became a club banger but also made waves in the mainstream music scene, propelling Rusko to new heights.

# BRINGING DUBSTEP TO THE MASSES

Another hit single that brought Rusko widespread acclaim was "Woo Boost," released in 2010. This track showcased his prowess in creating infectious dubstep anthems that resonated with fans around the world. With its addictive hooks, mind-bending drops, and a relentless groove, "Woo Boost" became an instant favorite among electronic music enthusiasts. Its success on the charts solidified Rusko's position as a leading figure in the dubstep genre.

But Rusko's chart success didn't stop there. He continued to release hit after hit, each one showcasing his ability to push boundaries and captivate listeners. "Hold On" featuring Amber Coffman, released in 2009, electrified dancefloors and climbed up the charts, cementing its place as one of Rusko's most iconic tracks. Its infectious melody, combined with Coffman's soulful vocals, created a blend of euphoria and energy that was impossible to resist.

In addition to these signature tracks, Rusko also collaborated with other artists to create chart-topping hits. His collaboration with British rapper and producer Example, "Dirty Dirty," was a commercial success, reaching the top of the charts in the UK. This high-energy track combined Rusko's production prowess with Example's slick rhymes, resulting in a dynamic and infectious hit.

The chart success of Rusko's singles can be attributed to several factors. Firstly, his ability to craft infectious melodies and captivating beats that resonate with a wide audience was undoubtedly a key factor in his chart domination. His unique sound, characterized by heavy basslines and intricate production, set him apart from his peers and made him a standout artist in the electronic music scene.

Furthermore, Rusko's skill in blending genres and styles played a crucial role in his chart success. He seamlessly integrated elements of dubstep, hip-hop, reggae, and more, creating a sound that appealed to a diverse range of listeners. This versatility allowed him to transcend genre boundaries and attract a wider fanbase, resulting in increased chart success.

Moreover, Rusko's energetic and captivating live performances further propelled his chart success. His ability to connect with the audience and create an immersive experience elevated his music beyond the realms of studio recordings. This connection with his fans translated into increased sales and streaming numbers, ultimately contributing to his presence on the charts.

In conclusion, Rusko's chart success can be attributed to his ability to create infectious tracks that resonated with a diverse audience. His unique sound, blending elements of dubstep, hip-hop, and more, set him apart from his peers, allowing him to climb the charts and solidify his position as a leading figure in the electronic music scene. Through hit singles like "Cockney Thug," "Woo Boost," and collaborations with other artists, Rusko's impact on the charts is undeniable, cementing his legacy as a chart-topping sensation.

So, grab your dancing shoes and turn up the volume because Rusko's hit singles are about to transport you to another dimension - a dimension where chart success and sonic brilliance collide. Get ready to be captivated as we delve deeper into the rise of Rusko in the next chapter of this captivating biography.

## Controversies and Backlash

Controversy seems to follow ambitious artists like a shadow, ready to pounce at the faintest sign of audacity. Rusko, with his innovative approach to dubstep, was no exception. As he pushed the boundaries of the genre, he met with both admiration and disdain, turning heads and raising eyebrows along the way. In this chapter, we delve into the controversies and backlash that accompanied Rusko's rise to stardom, exposing the challenges he faced in maintaining his creative integrity.

### Dubstep's Divisive Reception

Dubstep, as a relatively new genre in the early 2000s, polarized music enthusiasts. Its heavy basslines, syncopated rhythms, and experimental sound design were not easily digestible by the mainstream audience. Rusko, with his signature blend of dubstep, reggae, and jungle influences, was pushing the envelope even further.

Critics argued that his music lacked melody and was overtaken by relentless bass drops. They dismissed his compositions as noise and accused him of sacrificing musicality for the sake of creating outrageously filthy beats. Conservative music purists decried his deviation from traditional structures and dismissed his work as a passing fad.

### The Commercialization Debate

As Rusko's dubstep gained more attention and fans, the debate about commercialization reared its head. Some loyal fans felt that he was "selling out" by collaborating with more mainstream artists and producing tracks that appealed to a wider audience. They argued that his music became diluted, losing the raw and edgy quality that defined his earlier work.

On the other hand, Rusko defended his choices, emphasizing the importance of growth and evolution as an artist. He believed that reaching a larger audience allowed him to explore new sonic territories without compromising his artistic integrity. However, this stance only fueled the fire, intensifying the backlash from his original fanbase.

## The Sound of Rebellion

Rusko's rebellious attitude and non-conformist approach to music made him a lightning rod for criticism. His unconventional use of dissonance, aggressive basslines, and distorted bass wobbles challenged the established norms of dubstep. Purists accused him of diluting the genre, watering it down for mass consumption, and abandoning its underground roots.

Yet, Rusko's unapologetic demeanor only seemed to galvanize his supporters, attracting a new generation of fans who reveled in his audacious style. These fans connected with the rebellious nature of his music and relished in the energy and vibrancy it brought to their lives.

## Navigating the Backlash

Facing an onslaught of criticism, Rusko found himself at a crossroads. Should he cater to the demands of his original fanbase and stay true to his underground roots? Or should he embrace the commercial opportunities that presented themselves and potentially reach new heights of success?

Rusko, ever the risk-taker, found a delicate balance between the two. He remained true to his sound, continuing to produce tracks with his signature energy and creativity. At the same time, he allowed himself to explore new avenues and collaborate with diverse artists, expanding his sonic repertoire.

## Triumphs Amidst Adversity

Despite the controversies and backlash, Rusko's talent and determination continued to shine. His infectious beats and electrifying performances won over new audiences, helping propel dubstep into the mainstream. Furthermore, his success inspired a new wave of electronic artists to experiment and push the boundaries of their respective genres.

By staying true to himself and refusing to be confined by expectations, Rusko became a symbol of artistic independence. His ability to weather the storm of controversies and remain relevant in an ever-changing music landscape solidified his place in the annals of sonic history.

## Navigating Controversies with Style

Controversies and backlash are inherent in the world of creative expression. Rusko's journey serves as a testament to the resilience needed to overcome adversity while staying true to one's artistic vision. For aspiring artists, the key lies in embracing criticism as a catalyst for growth, not as a deterrent.

Amidst the controversies and backlash, Rusko's journey stands as an inspiration for artists who dare to challenge the status quo. By embracing one's uniqueness and navigating the treacherous waters of artistic criticism, true sonic revolutions can occur. Rusko's story is a living testament to the enduring power of creativity, resilience, and staying true to one's artistic vision.

## Evolution of Live Performances

The evolution of Rusko's live performances is a testament to his innovative spirit and his constant desire to push the boundaries of sonic experimentation. In this section, we will explore how Rusko transformed the live music experience, creating unforgettable performances that captivated audiences around the world.

### Forging a Unique Identity

One of the key elements that set Rusko apart from other artists was his ability to forge a unique identity in his live performances. From the early days of his career, Rusko understood the importance of creating an immersive experience for his fans. He wanted his performances to be more than just a concert – he wanted them to be a sonic journey that would leave a lasting impression.

To achieve this, Rusko embraced a combination of visual and audio elements, blending his signature electronic beats with stunning visuals and mesmerizing light shows. He carefully curated a stage presence that was both energetic and engaging, captivating the audience from the moment he stepped on stage.

### Hit Singles and Chart Success

As Rusko's popularity grew, so did the demand for his live performances. With the success of his hit singles such as "Cockney Thug" and "Woo Boost," Rusko found himself headlining major festivals and selling out shows worldwide. This newfound success placed him in the spotlight and made his live performances highly anticipated events.

Rusko understood the importance of delivering a show that lived up to the hype. His live performances became showcases of his chart-topping hits, with each song carefully choreographed to create a seamless flow of energy and excitement. From the moment the first beat dropped, the crowd would be on their feet, dancing and chanting along to every word.

## Controversies and Backlash

With success often comes controversy, and Rusko was not immune to its effects. As dubstep started to gain mainstream popularity, there were critics who accused Rusko of selling out and diluting the genre. Some dubstep purists felt that his live performances were too "pop-oriented" and lacked the raw underground energy that characterized the early days of the genre.

However, Rusko remained unfazed by the backlash. He believed that music should constantly evolve, and that live performances were the perfect platform for experimentation and exploration. Instead of conforming to expectations, he continued to innovate and push the boundaries of what a live dubstep performance could be.

## Evolution of Live Performances

Rusko's live performances evolved with every new project and collaboration. He constantly sought ways to elevate the live experience, incorporating new technologies and techniques to create a truly immersive sonic journey for his audience.

One of Rusko's notable contributions to the evolution of live performances was his integration of live instrumentation alongside electronic beats. He recognized the power of blending the organic and the synthetic, creating a dynamic and multi-dimensional sound that transcended traditional genres.

Another aspect that set Rusko's live performances apart was his use of live sampling and remixing. He would often take fan-favorite tracks and give them a fresh twist, weaving them seamlessly into his sets. This not only added a sense of spontaneity and excitement but also showcased Rusko's impeccable skills as a live performer.

## Dubstep's Influence on Popular Culture

Rusko's evolution of live performances not only had an impact on the electronic music scene but also on popular culture as a whole. As his live shows became more renowned, they attracted the attention of a broader audience, transcending the boundaries of the dubstep genre.

Rusko's live performances influenced visual artists, filmmakers, and even fashion designers. His incorporation of stunning visuals and immersive lighting created a new standard for live performances, inspiring artists in various disciplines to think outside the box and push the boundaries of their own respective crafts.

The impact of dubstep, and Rusko's live performances in particular, can still be felt in contemporary music and entertainment. The fusion of electronic beats, live instrumentation, and captivating visuals that Rusko pioneered continues to shape the way artists approach live performances to this day.

In conclusion, Rusko's evolution of live performances showcases his relentless pursuit of innovation and his commitment to creating a truly immersive and unforgettable experience for his fans. His ability to blend different elements and push the boundaries of sonic exploration has left a lasting impact on the electronic music scene and popular culture as a whole. As we dive deeper into Rusko's trials and triumphs, we will further explore the legacy he has built through his unparalleled live performances.

## Dominating the Festival Circuit

### Headlining Major Festivals

When it comes to the world of music, there are few accomplishments more prestigious than headlining major festivals. It's a defining moment in any artist's career, marking a transition from being an up-and-coming talent to becoming a sonic legend. Rusko's journey to this pinnacle of success was nothing short of remarkable. In this section, we'll explore how Rusko cemented his status as a festival headliner and left an indelible mark on the live music scene.

### Seizing the Spotlight

Rusko's rise to festival headliner status was not an overnight success. It was the culmination of years of hard work, dedication, and unwavering passion for his craft. As his reputation grew within the electronic music community, promoters began to take notice of his unique sound and dynamic stage presence.

One of the pivotal moments in Rusko's career came when he was offered a spot at a smaller, local music festival. Instead of shying away from the opportunity, he embraced it wholeheartedly. Rusko saw it as a chance to prove himself and showcase his talent to a wider audience. And he didn't disappoint.

His electrifying performance and infectious energy ignited the crowd, leaving everyone in awe of his abilities. From that moment on, Rusko's journey to headlining major festivals had begun.

### Climbing the Festival Ladder

With his foot in the door, Rusko set out to conquer the festival circuit. He tirelessly performed at every opportunity that came his way, slowly but surely climbing the ranks. Each performance was a chance to expand his fanbase, leaving a lasting impression on festival-goers and industry insiders alike.

As Rusko's popularity grew, so did his presence at festivals. He transitioned from playing early afternoon sets on smaller stages to commanding prime-time slots on the main stage. This meteoric rise was a testament to his talent, hard work, and ability to connect with a diverse audience.

## Taking Festivals by Storm

Rusko's headlining performances became legendary, setting the stage ablaze and leaving audiences craving more. His mastery of mixing and seamless transitions between genres created an unparalleled experience for festival-goers.

One of the secrets to Rusko's success was his ability to adapt his sound to the festival atmosphere. He expertly blended his signature dubstep beats with elements of drum and bass, reggae, and hip-hop to create a high-energy set that appealed to a wide range of musical tastes.

But it wasn't just Rusko's music that captivated audiences. His stage presence was magnetic, commanding attention from the moment he stepped on stage. From his infectious smile to his dance moves that seemed to defy gravity, Rusko knew how to engage the crowd and create an unforgettable experience.

## Pushing the Boundaries

As Rusko's reputation as a festival headliner grew, so did his ambition to push the boundaries of live music performance. He constantly sought innovative ways to enhance the festival experience, incorporating cutting-edge technology and visual effects into his sets.

One of his most memorable performances was at the renowned Electric Daisy Carnival. Rusko went above and beyond, bringing a team of visual artists and designers to create a mind-blowing spectacle of lights, lasers, and 3D projections. The result was a multi-sensory extravaganza that transported festival-goers to another dimension.

But it wasn't just about the spectacle. Rusko understood the importance of connecting with his audience on a personal level. He would often jump into the crowd, sharing the raw energy and excitement that reverberated throughout the festival grounds. This genuine interaction created an intimate bond between Rusko and his fans, solidifying his status as a beloved festival headliner.

## Dubstep's Festival Legacy

Rusko's ascent to festival headliner status coincided with the golden age of dubstep, a genre that dominated the electronic music scene in the late 2000s and early 2010s. His electrifying performances not only showcased his talent but also helped solidify dubstep's place in the festival landscape.

By headlining major festivals, Rusko played a pivotal role in bringing dubstep to the masses. His immersive and boundary-pushing sets paved the way for other dubstep artists to grace the main stages of festivals around the world. This marked a significant shift in the perception of the genre, elevating it from underground subculture to mainstream phenomenon.

## Conclusion - Rusko's Festival Reign

In conclusion, Rusko's journey to headlining major festivals is a testament to his talent, perseverance, and unwavering dedication to his craft. His electrifying performances and unique sound captured the hearts of festival-goers, leaving an indelible mark on the live music scene.

Through his captivating stage presence, seamless genre blending, and boundary-pushing performances, Rusko redefined what it means to be a festival headliner. He not only entertained the masses but also inspired a new generation of artists to push the limits of their creativity and create unforgettable live experiences.

Rusko's legacy as a festival headliner will continue to resonate throughout the music industry, inspiring and influencing future generations of sonic rebels. From humble beginnings to becoming a sonic legend, Rusko's journey is a testament to the power of passion and the enduring impact of live music.

## Unforgettable Performances

Ah, the unforgettable performances of Rusko! These were the moments that made the crowds go wild, the dance floors quake, and the music industry take notice. Rusko had an uncanny ability to captivate audiences with his unique blend of dubstep and energetic stage presence. From large festivals to intimate club shows, every performance was an experience that left a lasting impression on all who were lucky enough to witness his sonic magic.

One unforgettable performance that comes to mind is Rusko's headlining set at the prestigious Coachella Music Festival. The anticipation was palpable as the crowd eagerly awaited his arrival on stage. The atmosphere was electric, the energy contagious. And when Rusko finally took the stage, he unleashed a sonic assault that sent shockwaves through the desert air.

The set was a perfect balance of heavy bass drops, intricate melodies, and infectious rhythms. The crowd was in a frenzy, jumping, dancing, and losing themselves in the music. Rusko's stage presence was larger than life, as he moved and grooved to the beat, his charisma radiating from every pore. The unity between artist and audience was undeniable, and it was clear that Rusko was in his element.

But it wasn't just the music that made this performance unforgettable. Rusko had a knack for creating visually stunning experiences that complemented his sonic creations. The stage was adorned with an array of colorful lights, lasers, and smoke, creating a mesmerizing visual spectacle. It was as if the music and the visuals were in perfect harmony, amplifying each other's impact.

As the set progressed, Rusko continued to push the boundaries of what was possible in a live performance. He seamlessly blended tracks together, creating a seamless journey through his sonic universe. The crowd responded with equal enthusiasm, feeding off the energy that Rusko exuded from the stage.

And it wasn't just the big festival stages where Rusko's performances shone. He was equally at home in smaller, more intimate venues, where he could connect with the crowd on a more personal level. One particular show at a renowned underground club stands out in my memory. The venue was packed to the brim with die-hard fans eagerly awaiting Rusko's arrival.

When he finally took the stage, it was as if time stood still. The room was transformed into a swirling vortex of sound and movement. There was an undeniable intimacy in the air, as Rusko's music reverberated through the walls, creating a palpable connection between artist and audience. It was a truly transcendental experience, where the barriers between performer and spectator dissolved, and everyone became a part of something greater than themselves.

But Rusko's performances were not just about entertainment—they were also about pushing the boundaries of what was possible in live music. He was a true innovator, constantly experimenting with new techniques and technologies to create truly groundbreaking performances. One example of this was his use of live visuals, where he would manipulate visuals in real-time, creating a mesmerizing visual accompaniment to his music.

In conclusion, Rusko's unforgettable performances were a testament to his talent, creativity, and sheer passion for making music. Whether he was playing to thousands at a major festival or a few hundred in a small club, Rusko always gave his all, leaving the crowd in awe and craving for more. His performances were not just concerts; they were transformative experiences that left a lasting impact on all who had the privilege of witnessing them. And his legacy continues to inspire and influence artists to this day. So, let us raise our glasses and toast to Rusko, the sonic rebel who forever changed the game. Cheers!

## Pushing the Boundaries of Live Music

In the world of music, there are those who follow trends and play it safe, and then there are those who break free from the constraints of convention and push the boundaries of what is possible. Rusko falls into the latter category, a sonic pioneer who has redefined live performances and taken audiences on a journey unlike anything they have ever experienced before.

### Embracing Technology and Innovation

Rusko's quest to push the boundaries of live music begins with his embrace of technology and innovation. He has always been at the forefront of incorporating cutting-edge technology into his performances, constantly seeking new ways to enhance the sonic experience for his fans.

One of the ways Rusko has achieved this is through the use of live looping. By utilizing loop pedals and other looping devices, he is able to create intricate, layered compositions in real-time during his performances. This allows him to build up complex soundscapes on the fly, adding layer upon layer of music to create a truly immersive experience.

In addition to live looping, Rusko has also experimented with the use of custom-built instruments and controllers. He has worked closely with instrument designers and technologists to create unique instruments that allow him to manipulate sound in new and exciting ways. From modified synthesizers to MIDI controllers with custom mappings, Rusko is constantly pushing the boundaries of what is possible with live instrumentation.

### Blurring the Lines Between DJ and Live Act

Traditionally, electronic music artists have been categorized as either DJs or live acts. DJs typically rely on pre-recorded tracks and mix them together in real-time, while live acts perform with instruments and create music on the spot. However, Rusko refuses to be confined by these labels and has carved out a unique space for himself that blurs the lines between the two.

In his live performances, Rusko seamlessly combines elements of DJing and live instrumentation. He incorporates his signature live looping techniques with carefully curated pre-recorded tracks, allowing him to create a dynamic and ever-evolving set that bridges the gap between the spontaneity of a live act and the precision of a DJ.

By breaking free from the constraints of traditional categorization, Rusko has created a truly immersive and captivating live experience that keeps audiences on their toes and leaves them craving more.

## Creating a Visual Spectacle

What sets Rusko's live performances apart from the rest is his ability to create a visual spectacle that complements the sonic journey he takes his audience on. He understands that music is a multi-sensory experience, and he goes above and beyond to engage all the senses during his shows.

Rusko's stage setup is a work of art in itself. Elaborate lighting rigs, video projections, and synchronized visuals create a mesmerizing backdrop that enhances the sonic experience. From pulsating lights that match the beat of the music to carefully choreographed visuals that tell a story, every aspect of the visual production is thoughtfully designed to immerse the audience in Rusko's sonic dimensions.

## Exceeding Expectations and Redefining Live Music

Rusko's commitment to pushing the boundaries of live music has not only elevated the electronic music scene, but it has also inspired a new generation of artists to think outside the box. By embracing technology, blurring the lines between DJing and live performance, and creating a visual spectacle, he has created a new standard for what a live music experience can be.

But pushing boundaries is not without its challenges. Rusko has faced criticism and skepticism from those who resist change and innovation. However, he remains undeterred, continually evolving his sound and pushing himself to explore new frontiers.

In conclusion, Rusko's relentless pursuit of pushing the boundaries of live music has transformed the electronic music landscape. Through his innovative use of technology, blurring of traditional categorizations, and creation of immersive visual spectacles, he has redefined what it means to experience live music. His influence will be felt for generations to come, inspiring musicians to continue pushing the limits of what is possible. So, buckle up and get ready to be transported into the sonic dimensions of Rusko's world.

## Dubstep's Influence on Popular Culture

Dubstep, with its deep basslines and heavy drops, has carved a unique space for itself within the realm of electronic music. Born from the underground music scene in the UK, dubstep exploded onto the mainstream stage, captivating audiences worldwide with its gritty sound and infectious energy. In this section, we explore the profound influence of dubstep on popular culture, from its impact on other music genres to its infiltration into movies, commercials, and even fashion.

## Transforming the Music Landscape

Dubstep's rise to prominence brought about a seismic shift in the music landscape, pushing boundaries and blurring genre lines. Its heavy basslines, syncopated rhythms, and futuristic soundscapes found favor with not only EDM enthusiasts but also musicians outside the electronic sphere.

One of the most notable impacts of dubstep on popular culture was its fusion with mainstream pop music. Artists like Rihanna, Beyoncé, and Katy Perry incorporated dubstep elements into their tracks, infusing their music with an edgy and contemporary vibe. The incorporation of dubstep-influenced drops and wobbly basslines into these chart-topping hits exposed a wider audience to the genre, leading to its further proliferation.

Furthermore, the influence of dubstep extended beyond the realm of pop music. It found a natural synergy with hip-hop and rap, leading to the emergence of subgenres like trapstep and drill. Artists such as Skrillex, Diplo, and Flosstradamus successfully bridged the gap between dubstep and hip-hop, resulting in truly groundbreaking collaborations and genre-bending tracks.

## Dubstep's Cinematic Impact

Dubstep's unparalleled ability to evoke intense emotions and create a sense of urgency made it a fitting companion for the silver screen. Filmmakers quickly recognized the potential of dubstep to elevate action sequences and heighten suspense, resulting in its inclusion in numerous movies, TV shows, and video games.

Dubstep's impact on popular culture is perhaps best exemplified by its role in the soundtrack for the blockbuster film "The Great Gatsby." The high-energy, bass-heavy remix of Beyoncé's "Crazy in Love" by producer Emeli Sandé perfectly captured the film's contemporary take on the Jazz Age. This juxtaposition of temporal elements, blending the old with the new, contributed to the film's overall aesthetic and cultural resonance.

Dubstep's influence has also permeated the gaming industry, with its distinctive sound often used to enhance the immersive experience of video games. Titles such as "Fortnite," "Need for Speed," and "Far Cry" have incorporated dubstep tracks into their soundtracks, matching the intensity of gameplay and heightening the adrenaline rush for players.

## Fashion and Dubstep's Aesthetic

The impact of dubstep extends beyond just its sonic influence; it has also made a significant impact on fashion. The distinctive style associated with the genre, characterized by its dark, futuristic, and avant-garde aesthetic, rapidly gained traction in popular culture.

Dubstep's fashion influence can be seen in the emergence of "cybergoth" and "steampunk" subcultures, both of which draw inspiration from the genre's electronic soundscape. These subcultures combine elements of sci-fi, post-apocalyptic aesthetics, and DIY fashion, resulting in striking visual representations deeply intertwined with the dubstep experience.

In addition, dubstep's influence has transcended subcultures and inspired mainstream fashion as well. High fashion designers have incorporated dubstep-inspired elements such as metallic fabrics, asymmetrical cuts, and futuristic designs into their collections. The bold and boundary-pushing nature of dubstep aligns perfectly with the avant-garde ethos of the fashion industry, creating a symbiotic relationship between the two realms.

## Problem: Analyzing Dubstep's Socio-cultural Impact

To truly understand the influence of dubstep on popular culture, it is essential to conduct a comprehensive analysis of its socio-cultural impact. As a student of musicology or cultural studies, you are tasked with exploring the broader implications of the genre's success.

**Problem:** Analyze the socio-cultural impact of dubstep on popular culture. How has the genre influenced societal norms, fashion, entertainment, and the music industry as a whole? Provide specific examples and identify any criticisms or controversies associated with dubstep's influence.

**Solution:** To tackle this problem, you would need to conduct extensive research on the rise of dubstep and its far-reaching effects on various aspects of popular culture. Start by examining the genre's evolution, its fusion with other genres, and its prominent role in pop music and hip-hop. Explore how dubstep's aesthetic has influenced fashion trends and subcultures, and delve into its presence in movies, TV shows, and video games. Finally, consider any criticisms or controversies surrounding dubstep's impact, such as accusations of cultural appropriation or the dilution of the genre's original sound.

# Chapter Three: Trials and Triumphs

## The Dark Side of Success

### Struggles with Substance Abuse

The journey of Rusko hasn't always been smooth sailing. Behind the scenes of his meteoric rise to fame, he faced a tumultuous battle with substance abuse that threatened to overshadow his immense talent and potential. This section delves into the darkest chapter of Rusko's life, shedding light on the struggles he faced, the impact it had on his music career, and his path to recovery.

### The Lure of Escapism

For Rusko, the pressures of fame and the demanding music industry served as fertile grounds for the development of his substance abuse problem. Adoring fans, constant touring, and the need to meet ever-increasing expectations took their toll on his mental and emotional well-being. Faced with this overwhelming reality, Rusko sought solace in substances as a means of escape.

### The Downward Spiral

As Rusko's substance abuse escalated, it began to infiltrate all aspects of his life. His once-thriving career started to crumble, plagued by missed gigs, canceled shows, and an inability to meet professional commitments. Collaborations that were once eagerly anticipated now became a source of disappointment and frustration. Behind closed doors, his personal relationships suffered as well, strained by the grip of addiction.

### The Intervention

Amidst the chaos and turmoil, a crucial turning point came in the form of an intervention from close friends and family. Recognizing the severity of Rusko's addiction and the dire consequences it posed, they staged an intervention that would change the course of his life. Emotional confrontations, heartfelt pleas, and genuine concern propelled Rusko towards seeking help.

### The Road to Recovery

Recovery from substance abuse is a challenging journey, and Rusko's path was no exception. The musician committed himself to a comprehensive rehabilitation program that included intensive therapy, counseling, and support from addiction specialists. Breaking the cycle of addiction required tremendous effort, summoning every ounce of Rusko's determination and resilience.

### Rediscovering Self and Passion

As Rusko progressed through his recovery, he was faced with the task of rediscovering himself and his passion for music. Sobriety served as the catalyst for a newfound clarity, enabling him to reconnect with his artistry on a profound level. Through introspection and self-reflection, he channeled his experiences, emotions, and struggles into his music.

### The Power of Music in Healing

Music became Rusko's anchor during his journey to sobriety. Through his compositions, he found an outlet for expression, a cathartic release that allowed him to process the depths of his addiction. This transformational experience imbued his music with a raw and authentic quality that resonated deeply with his fans, creating a profound connection.

### Advocacy for Addiction Recovery

Inspired by his own battle, Rusko became an advocate for addiction recovery, using his platform to raise awareness, destigmatize addiction, and promote access to resources for those in need. Through interviews, public appearances, and partnerships with organizations focused on addiction support, he championed the cause and inspired hope in others facing similar struggles.

## A Story of Triumph

Rusko's struggles with substance abuse are an integral part of his story, highlighting the resilience of the human spirit and the power of determination. His journey from the darkest depths of addiction to a place of recovery and redemption serves as an inspiration to fans and aspiring musicians alike. It is a testament to the transformative power of self-belief, support, and the unyielding pursuit of personal growth.

## Caveats and Lessons

Rusko's battle with substance abuse serves as a cautionary tale, reminding us of the perils that can come hand in hand with success and fame. It underscores the importance of mental health care, community support, and fostering a culture of understanding and empathy within the music industry. It is a stark reminder that behind the glitz and glamour lies a human being, grappling with their own demons and vulnerability.

## Behind the Music

In a revealing interview, Rusko shares his experiences and insights into his struggles with substance abuse, shedding light on the challenges he faced and the impact it had on his music. This intimate conversation offers a unique perspective, humanizing the artist and emphasizing the significance of his journey to recovery.

## Discussion Questions

1. How do you think the pressures of the music industry contribute to the prevalence of substance abuse among artists? 2. What role can the music industry play in supporting artists struggling with addiction? 3. How do you think Rusko's personal experiences have influenced the direction and themes of his music? 4. In what ways can society contribute to the destigmatization of addiction and encourage a more empathetic approach towards those in recovery? 5. How can artists like Rusko use their platform to raise awareness about addiction and promote resources for recovery?

## Further Resources

1. "Scar Tissue" by Anthony Kiedis: This memoir provides an insight into the personal struggles of the Red Hot Chili Peppers frontman and his battle with

addiction. 2. MusiCares: A foundation established by the Recording Academy that provides resources and support for musicians in times of need, including addiction recovery programs. 3. National Helpline: 1-800-662-HELP (4357) - A confidential, free 24/7 helpline offering information and treatment referrals for individuals facing substance abuse issues in the United States.

Remember, addiction is a complex issue, and seeking professional help is essential for anyone struggling with substance abuse.

## Personal and Professional Challenges

Life as a musician is not always glitter and gold, and Rusko's journey is no exception. Alongside the successes and triumphs, he faced a series of personal and professional challenges that put his resilience and determination to the test. In this chapter, we delve into the obstacles he encountered on his path to sonic greatness.

### Struggles with Substance Abuse

Behind the scenes of the music industry, there lies a darker side, one that often tempts and ensnares artists on their rise to fame. Rusko found himself grappling with the allure of substances, seeking solace in drugs and alcohol as he dealt with the pressures of stardom. The constant demand for performances, the relentless touring schedules, and the expectation to always deliver an exceptional experience took their toll on his mental and physical well-being.

The impact of substance abuse on Rusko's personal life and creative output cannot be overlooked. It affected his relationships with loved ones, strained collaborations, and hindered his ability to maintain a consistent work ethic. The music industry is notorious for its excessive party culture, and Rusko found himself caught in its destructive grip.

*Troubles that arise from a combination of drugs and alcohol are not exclusive to musicians. In fact, studies have shown that substance abuse affects individuals from all walks of life, particularly in creative fields where self-expression and experimentation are commonplace.*

**Example Problem:**

Rusko has realized that his substance abuse is hindering his creativity and damaging his health. He decides to seek help and undergo a rehabilitation program. During his treatment, he faces the challenge of rebuilding not only his physical and mental well-being but also his career.

**Solution:**

Rusko's decision to enter rehab is a crucial turning point in his life. It allows him to confront his addiction head-on, breaking free from its grip and regaining control over his life. The rehabilitation process involves detoxification, therapy sessions, and support from professionals who specialize in addiction recovery.

As Rusko progresses through treatment, he gradually starts to see positive changes in his creativity and music-making. The clear mind and newfound clarity allow him to tap into emotions and experiences that were previously clouded by substance abuse. With each passing day, he regains confidence in his abilities and rediscovers the joy of creating music.

*Recovering from substance abuse is a complex and challenging journey that requires dedication, support, and a strong sense of self-awareness. The road to recovery is different for everyone, but seeking professional help and building a support system of friends and family is crucial.*

## Personal and Professional Challenges

Beyond substance abuse, Rusko faced a series of personal and professional challenges that tested his resilience and determination. The demanding nature of the music industry often took a toll on his mental health and strained his personal relationships. The constant pressure to create groundbreaking music, deal with the pressures of fame, and maintain a rigorous touring schedule required immense strength and perseverance.

Moreover, the ever-changing dynamics of the music industry presented its own set of challenges. The emergence of new genres, evolving audience tastes, and shifting market trends forced Rusko to adapt and reinvent himself continuously. It was not always easy to strike a balance between staying true to his artistic vision and meeting commercial expectations.

*Navigating the music industry is a delicate balance between artistry and business acumen. Artists must constantly adapt to stay relevant, while also staying true to their own unique sound and style.*

**Example Problem:**

Rusko finds himself in a creative rut, struggling to come up with new material that satisfies both his artistic instincts and his audience's expectations. He's torn between maintaining his signature sound and exploring new musical territories. How can Rusko overcome this challenge and regain his creative spark?

**Solution:**

To overcome this challenge, Rusko takes a step back and reconnects with his musical roots. He immerses himself in a diverse range of genres and styles, seeking inspiration from artists who have successfully blended innovation with familiarity.

Rusko recognizes the importance of balance, understanding that his uniqueness lies in his ability to push boundaries while staying true to his sonic identity.

Additionally, Rusko begins collaborating with artists from various genres, allowing their fresh perspectives to ignite his creativity. By embracing new collaborations, he opens himself up to new possibilities and experiences that spark his creative flame.

Ultimately, Rusko finds the courage to embrace change and experimentation without losing sight of his artistic essence. He rediscovers his passion for music and unleashes a new wave of sonic innovation that captivates his audience and redefines his sound.

*Creativity is not a static entity but rather a constantly evolving process. It requires artists to embrace challenges, take risks, and continually push the boundaries of their own comfort zones.*

## Rediscovering Passion for Music

Amidst personal and professional challenges, Rusko embarked on a journey to rediscover his true passion for music. He realized that success and fame alone cannot sustain a fulfilling career; it is the love for music that provides the enduring motivation to push through adversity.

Through introspection and self-reflection, Rusko found himself reconnecting with the very essence of why he started making music in the first place. He recognized the power of his own voice and the impact it could have on those who listened. This realization fueled his determination to overcome the obstacles that stood in his way.

*Rediscovering one's passion is a deeply personal and transformative process. It requires self-reflection, a willingness to confront one's fears and insecurities, and the courage to embrace personal growth.*

**Example Problem:**

Rusko is faced with creative burnout, feeling uninspired and detached from his music. How can he reignite his passion and find renewed motivation in his art?

**Solution:**

To reignite his passion for music, Rusko takes a step back from the spotlight and reconnects with his innate creativity. He explores new artistic avenues, embracing other forms of self-expression such as visual arts or writing. This allows him to approach music from a fresh perspective and discover new sources of inspiration.

Rusko also seeks out collaborations with artists he deeply admires, fostering an environment of mutual creativity and support. By surrounding himself with like-minded individuals, he finds motivation and encouragement to push his artistic boundaries.

Most importantly, Rusko takes time for self-care and mental rejuvenation. He prioritizes his physical and mental well-being, recognizing that a healthy mind and body are essential for maintaining passion and creativity.

Through these deliberate actions, Rusko gradually finds himself falling back in love with music. He embraces the ups and downs of his journey, finding solace in the knowledge that true fulfillment lies in the enduring passion he has for his craft.

*Passion for music is a flame that must be nurtured, protected, and allowed to grow. It requires self-reflection, adaptation, and perseverance in the face of challenges. Rediscovering one's passion is a powerful source of inspiration and the key to unlocking one's full potential as an artist.*

## Rehab and Road to Recovery

The path to success is often littered with obstacles and challenges, and Rusko's journey was no exception. In this chapter, we take a closer look at the trials and tribulations that Rusko faced during his rise to stardom. One pivotal moment in Rusko's life was his battle with substance abuse, which took a toll on both his personal and professional life. However, it was during this period that he found the strength to seek help and embark on a journey of recovery.

## Facing the Demons

Like many artists who find themselves in the spotlight, Rusko's success brought with it a fair share of struggles. The pressures of fame and the fast-paced music industry took a toll on his mental health, leading him down a dark path of substance abuse. This battle not only affected his music but threatened to consume his life entirely.

Despite the challenges he faced, Rusko mustered the courage to confront his demons head-on. He recognized that in order to continue pursuing his passion for music, he needed to prioritize his well-being. This self-awareness was a crucial first step towards his journey to recovery.

## The Turning Point

The road to recovery is often filled with twists and turns, setbacks, and triumphs. For Rusko, the turning point came when he made the difficult decision to enter a rehabilitation program. This step required immense strength and vulnerability, as he faced the reality of his addiction and committed to making a change.

During his time in rehab, Rusko not only focused on overcoming his substance abuse but also worked on rebuilding his emotional and mental well-being. Through therapy, counseling, and self-reflection, he gained a deeper understanding of the underlying issues contributing to his addiction. This newfound awareness empowered him to confront and address these challenges head-on.

## Rediscovering the Passion

Rehabilitation marked a significant turning point in Rusko's life. As he started to regain control over his addiction, he also rediscovered his passion for music. The process of recovery allowed him to reconnect with his creativity and find a new sense of purpose.

During this period, Rusko channeled his emotions and experiences into his music. He used songwriting as a form of therapy, expressing his struggles and triumphs through powerful lyrics and melodies. The process not only helped him heal but also allowed him to create deeply personal and resonating music with his audience.

## Rebuilding Trust and Fanbase

Rebuilding trust is a crucial aspect of recovery, not only with oneself but also with others. Rusko knew that in order for his music career to thrive, he needed to gain the trust and support of his fans once again. He embarked on this journey with humility and transparency, addressing his struggles openly and honestly.

Through interviews, social media interactions, and heartfelt performances, Rusko shared his story of recovery, relatability, and resilience. He not only acknowledged his past mistakes but also showed a genuine commitment to changing his ways. This authenticity resonated with his fans, who rallied behind him and embraced his journey towards redemption.

## A Sonic Rebirth

Recovery marked a new chapter in Rusko's musical career. With a revived sense of purpose, he approached his craft with newfound enthusiasm and creativity. His experiences with addiction and the path to recovery allowed him to create music that was not only sonically innovative but also deeply introspective.

Rusko's music took on an entirely new dimension, with lyrics and melodies that reflected his personal growth and transformation. Through his artistry, he sought to inspire others who were grappling with similar challenges, offering them hope and showing them that a life beyond addiction was possible.

## Embracing Community and Support

No journey towards recovery is complete without the support and love of others. Rusko recognized the importance of surrounding himself with positive influences, both within the music industry and in his personal life. He sought out genuine connections and formed strong relationships with like-minded individuals who shared his commitment to personal growth and well-being.

In addition to seeking support, Rusko also became an advocate for addiction recovery, using his platform to raise awareness and destigmatize the issue. He collaborated with organizations and fellow artists on projects that aimed to provide resources and support for individuals battling addiction.

## A New Chapter Begins

Rusko's journey through rehab and recovery marked a significant turning point in his life and career. It was a period of growth, resilience, and self-discovery that allowed him to emerge stronger and more focused than ever before.

With a renewed sense of purpose, Rusko embraced the opportunity to continue creating music that pushed boundaries and resonated with his audience. He remained committed to his own personal growth and well-being, ensuring that his career would be sustained by an unwavering dedication to his craft and a commitment to maintaining a healthy and balanced lifestyle.

As Rusko began this new chapter, he did so with the knowledge that his experiences with addiction and recovery would forever shape his musical legacy. His story serves as a reminder that even in the face of adversity, it is possible to overcome one's demons and come out stronger on the other side.

## Rediscovering Passion for Music

After going through a tumultuous period in his life filled with ups and downs, Rusko found himself at a crossroads where he had to reevaluate his relationship with music. The once vibrant and passionate artist had lost his way, but deep inside, he knew that his love for music still burned. It was in this darkest hour that Rusko embarked on a journey of self-discovery, determined to rediscover his passion for the art that had shaped his life.

4.1.1 Struggles with Substance Abuse

Like many artists before him, Rusko found refuge in the escape that substances offered. However, this path took a toll on his personal and professional life, leading to a downward spiral. Substance abuse not only affected his health but also hindered his ability to create meaningful music. It was a wake-up call that forced him to confront his demons and make a choice – continue down this destructive path or find a way to rise above it.

#### 4.1.2 Personal and Professional Challenges

Apart from struggles with substance abuse, Rusko was also faced with personal and professional challenges that tested his resilience. The constant demands of the music industry and the pressure to produce hit after hit began to take a toll on his creativity and mental well-being. It felt like the spark that once ignited his passion had dimmed, and he found himself questioning his purpose as an artist.

#### 4.1.3 Rehab and Road to Recovery

In a moment of clarity, Rusko made the brave decision to seek help and checked himself into rehab. It was a pivotal moment that marked the beginning of his journey to recovery. Surrounded by a supportive network of professionals and loved ones, he faced the challenging process of detoxification and rehabilitation. Through therapy, self-reflection, and healing, Rusko gradually regained control of his life and rediscovered the importance of music in his journey.

#### 4.1.4 Rediscovering Passion for Music

As Rusko transitioned from rehab back into the real world, he found himself standing at the intersection of doubt and hope. It was during this pivotal moment that he stumbled upon something unexpected – a deep well of inspiration within him that had been dormant for far too long. Through introspection and soul-searching, Rusko began to reconnect with the essence of his artistry.

He delved into exploring different genres, pushing the boundaries of his sound, and experimenting with unconventional instruments and techniques. This newfound creative freedom allowed him to express his emotions on a deeper level and reignited his passion for music. Rusko's journey of rediscovery became a testament to the transformative power of art and its ability to bring light into the darkest corners of our lives.

To further push his boundaries, Rusko started collaborating with artists from diverse backgrounds, fusing different styles and influences into his music. These collaborations not only sparked fresh creative energy but also introduced Rusko to new perspectives and artistic approaches. It was through this process that he discovered a renewed sense of purpose – to use his music as a vehicle for self-expression and connection.

##### 4.1.4.1 Exploring New Sounds: The Fusion Experiment

Rusko's journey to rediscover his passion for music led him on a path of sonic exploration, unafraid to blend genres and experiment with unconventional soundscapes. He embraced the fusion of electronic elements with live instrumentation, creating a sonic tapestry that was both innovative and captivating.

The incorporation of organic elements brought an added layer of depth and authenticity to his music, captivating audiences and critics alike.

4.1.4.2 New Collaborations and Unexpected Projects

Collaborations became an integral part of Rusko's rediscovery. Working with artists from different musical backgrounds opened doors to uncharted territories, sparking creativity and inspiration. Unexpected projects emerged, bringing together seemingly disparate genres and creating a melting pot of sonic innovation. These collaborations not only challenged Rusko as an artist but also served as a bridge, connecting audiences from different musical spheres.

4.1.4.3 The Journey Towards Self-Acceptance

One of the most profound outcomes of Rusko's rediscovery of his passion for music was the journey towards self-acceptance. Through his struggles and triumphs, he realized that his art was a reflection of his own personal growth and experiences. Rusko embraced his past, flaws, and all, using them as fuel to create music that was honest, vulnerable, and resonated deeply with his audience.

The process of rediscovering his passion for music was not a linear one. It was marked by setbacks and moments of self-doubt. However, through perseverance and a relentless pursuit of authenticity, Rusko emerged as a stronger and more resilient artist.

As Rusko's story illustrates, the pursuit of passion is not always a smooth journey. It is one filled with obstacles, moments of self-discovery, and constant growth. But it is through these challenges that artists like Rusko are able to transform their craft, inspiring others to follow their dreams and find their own creative voices.

## Exercises

1. Reflect on a time when you felt a loss of passion for something you loved. What steps did you take to rediscover that passion? How did it impact your journey?

2. Research and listen to music from different genres that you are unfamiliar with. Take note of the elements that stand out to you and try to incorporate them into your own creative pursuits.

3. Collaborate with someone from a different artistic discipline or background. How does this collaboration influence your work and mindset? Explore the possibilities of merging different styles and techniques.

4. Experiment with unconventional instruments or techniques in your creative process. How does this change your perspective and approach to your craft?

5. Write a letter to your younger self, offering words of advice and encouragement during a challenging period of your life. Reflect on how that experience shaped you and how it can continue to inspire your creative journey.

Remember, the path to rediscovering passion may not always be linear, but it is through perseverance and self-exploration that true growth and artistic breakthroughs can occur. Embrace every step of the journey and let your passion guide you towards new dimensions of creativity.

# Reinventing Himself

## Return to the Spotlight

After a period of personal and professional challenges, Rusko found himself at a crossroads. Struggling with substance abuse and facing setbacks in his music career, he embarked on a journey to rediscover his passion for music and make a triumphant return to the spotlight.

## A Moment of Clarity

While battling his demons, Rusko had a moment of clarity that made him realize the importance of reclaiming his music career. He recognized that his talent and unique sound were too valuable to be overshadowed by personal struggles. This newfound determination served as the catalyst for his return to the spotlight.

## Reconnecting with the Music

To start his comeback, Rusko began by immersing himself in the music that had once brought him joy. He listened to a wide range of genres, from classical compositions to cutting-edge electronic tracks, allowing himself to explore new sounds and inspirations. This process helped him rediscover his artistic voice and paved the way for his triumphant return.

## Collaborations and Musical Reinvention

Rusko understood the power of collaboration and sought out opportunities to work with other artists who shared his passion for music. By joining forces with talented musicians from different genres, he was able to expand his sonic horizons and experiment with new styles. These collaborations not only showcased his versatility as an artist but also helped him gain fresh perspectives on his own music.

## Crafting a Comeback Sound

As Rusko worked on crafting his comeback sound, he faced the challenge of satisfying his loyal fanbase while also attracting new listeners. He strived to strike a balance between staying true to his signature dubstep roots and pushing the boundaries of his music. Through meticulous production techniques and a fearless approach to sonic experimentation, Rusko successfully carved out a unique sound that resonated with both old and new audiences.

## Embracing the Evolution of Dubstep

During his hiatus, the dubstep scene had undergone significant changes. Rusko made a conscious effort to familiarize himself with the new trends and innovations in the genre. He embraced the evolution of dubstep, incorporating elements of bass music, trap, and future beats into his own compositions. This adaptability helped him stay relevant and connect with a wider range of listeners.

## Connecting with the Fans

Rusko understood the importance of building a strong connection with his fans. He used social media platforms to engage with his followers, sharing behind-the-scenes footage, personal anecdotes, and sneak peeks of his upcoming projects. By inviting his fans into his creative process, he fostered a sense of intimacy and loyalty that fueled his comeback.

## Breaking the Mold

As he returned to the spotlight, Rusko challenged the conventional norms of live performances. He infused his shows with an electric energy, combining his pulsating beats with stunning visuals and immersive stage designs. Each performance became an unforgettable experience, pushing the boundaries of what was possible in live electronic music.

## Inspiring Others

Rusko's journey from personal struggles to musical redemption served as an inspiration to aspiring artists facing their own challenges. He openly shared his story of overcoming adversity, spreading a message of hope and resilience. Through his music and his words, he encouraged others to pursue their dreams fearlessly and to never let setbacks define them.

## Continuing the Legacy

The return to the spotlight was just the beginning of a new chapter in Rusko's career. With his newfound passion and a reinvigorated sense of purpose, he looked forward to exploring new frontiers in electronic music. His commitment to innovation and sonic experimentation promised to leave a lasting impact on the industry and inspire future generations of artists.

In conclusion, Rusko's return to the spotlight was a testament to his resilience, creativity, and unwavering love for music. Through collaborations, musical reinvention, and a dedication to connecting with his fans, he successfully reclaimed his place in the industry. His story serves as a reminder that even in the face of adversity, with passion and determination, one can overcome any challenge and shine brightly once again.

## Collaborations and Experimentation

Collaborations are like the secret sauce that adds flavor and depth to an artist's body of work. Rusko, being the sonic rebel that he is, has never shied away from exploring new musical territories and pushing the boundaries of electronic music. In this section, we delve into Rusko's notable collaborations and his daring experimentation that has left an indelible mark on the music industry.

### The Rise of Unlikely Collaborations

Rusko, with his innovative approach to music, has consistently sought out collaborations with artists from diverse backgrounds. One such unexpected partnership was with the likes of Skrillex, who at the time was relatively unknown. This unlikely pairing gave rise to the groundbreaking EP, "Scary Monsters and Nice Sprites," which went on to become a game-changer in the electronic music scene.

Their collaboration showcased a fusion of Rusko's dubstep roots with Skrillex's aggressive and energetic sound. The result was a sonic explosion that captivated audiences and propelled both artists to new heights. This collaboration not only solidified Rusko's reputation as a sonic pioneer but also helped Skrillex gain recognition and find his own distinct voice.

### Pushing the Boundaries

Experimentation is the lifeblood of any true artist, and Rusko is no exception. He constantly seeks to push the boundaries of electronic music by infusing elements from a wide range of genres. One of the notable influences in his experimentation was his exploration of reggae and dancehall.

Rusko's collaboration with Jamaican dancehall artist, Mr. Vegas, resulted in the infectious track "Woo Boost." This groundbreaking fusion of dubstep and dancehall showcased Rusko's ability to seamlessly blend diverse styles and create a sound that was both fresh and exhilarating.

Another intriguing collaboration was with Cypress Hill, the iconic hip-hop group. The track "Roll It, Light It" exemplifies Rusko's ability to bridge the gap between different genres, combining the hard-hitting beats of hip-hop with the gritty basslines of dubstep. This collaboration not only brought together two distinct musical worlds but also opened doors for a broader audience to experience the unique sonic landscape created by Rusko.

## A Sonic Playground

Rusko's collaborations serve as his playground, where he fearlessly experiments with sonic elements to create truly innovative and boundary-pushing music. One such example is his collaboration with the American rapper, Gucci Mane. On the track "Hold On," Rusko infused his signature dubstep sound with Gucci Mane's lyrical prowess, resulting in a track that defies categorization.

In his constant quest for sonic exploration, Rusko has also ventured into the realm of live instrumentation. His collaboration with the London Symphony Orchestra brought a sweeping cinematic quality to his music. The fusion of electronic beats with the soaring melodies of a full orchestra showcased Rusko's versatility and ability to adapt his sound in unconventional ways.

## Breaking Down Barriers

Rusko's collaborations not only break down genre barriers but also challenge the traditional notion of what defines electronic music. His partnership with the Scottish singer-songwriter, Emeli Sandé, on the track "Heaven" pushed the boundaries of electronic music by infusing it with soulful vocals and heartfelt lyrics. This collaboration demonstrated Rusko's ability to connect with listeners on an emotional level while maintaining his signature sonic innovation.

In his quest for musical experimentation, Rusko has also embraced the world of remixes. His collaboration with fellow dubstep producer, Caspa, on their joint remix of Adele's "Rolling in the Deep," exemplifies Rusko's ability to reimagine a chart-topping hit with his unique sonic perspective. This collaboration not only showcased his talent for transforming a song but also introduced a new audience to the world of electronic music.

Through his collaborations and fearless experimentation, Rusko has paved the way for a new generation of artists to push the boundaries of their own creativity. His willingness to venture into uncharted territory and merge genres has left an undeniable mark on the music industry, forever changing the sonic landscape and inspiring countless artists to follow in his footsteps.

So, whether it's collaborating with unlikely partners, pushing the boundaries of electronic music, or breaking down genre barriers, Rusko's bold experimentation continues to reshape the sonic landscape and leave an enduring influence on the world of music.

## Exercises

1. Choose a well-known song from a different genre and imagine a collaboration with Rusko. Describe how you think his unique sonic perspective could transform the song.

2. Research another notable collaboration in the electronic music world and analyze how the partnership influenced the development of both artists' careers.

3. Experiment with combining elements from different genres to create a unique sonic blend. Write a short piece of music that showcases your exploration and reflects the spirit of Rusko's experimentation.

4. Reflect on a time when you have collaborated with someone from a different background or expertise. Describe how the collaboration enriched your own creative process and what you learned from it.

Remember, collaborations and experimentation are all about breaking down barriers and exploring new possibilities. So, don't be afraid to think outside the box and let your creative instincts guide you. The sonic revolution begins with you!

## Embracing New Sounds

In the ever-evolving world of music, the ability to embrace new sounds is essential for artists to maintain relevance and push the boundaries of their creativity. Rusko, known for his groundbreaking contributions to the dubstep genre, has always been a pioneer in the exploration of new sonic landscapes. In this section, we delve into his journey of embracing new sounds and how it has shaped his musical career.

## Evolution as an Artist

As an artist, Rusko has never been content with staying within the confines of a single genre or style. He constantly seeks out new sounds and experiences to challenge himself artistically. This approach has led to his continual evolution and growth as a musician, as he consistently seeks to reinvent his sound and explore uncharted territories.

To embrace new sounds, Rusko actively immerses himself in different musical scenes and collaborates with artists from various genres and backgrounds. By doing so, he not only expands his own sonic palette but also brings fresh perspectives and influences into his music.

## Breaking Down Barriers

One of the ways Rusko has embraced new sounds is by breaking down barriers between different genres. He defies conventional classifications and seamlessly blends elements of dubstep, reggae, hip-hop, and electronica to create his unique fusion of sound.

By incorporating diverse musical influences, Rusko creates a rich and dynamic sonic experience that appeals to a wide audience. This innovative approach challenges traditional genre boundaries, encouraging listeners to explore new sounds and expand their musical horizons.

## Exploration of New Production Techniques

Embracing new sounds not only involves experimenting with different genres but also entails exploring new production techniques. Rusko has consistently pushed the boundaries of electronic music production, incorporating innovative methods to create distinctive and captivating soundscapes.

One example of Rusko's exploration of new production techniques is his use of futuristic synthesizers and cutting-edge software. By harnessing the power of technology, he is able to manipulate sounds, create unique textures, and craft immersive sonic experiences for his listeners.

## Musical Diversity and Hybridity

In embracing new sounds, Rusko recognizes the importance of musical diversity and hybridity. He actively seeks inspiration from a variety of cultural influences, infusing his music with elements from different parts of the world.

For instance, Rusko's collaboration with artists from diverse cultural backgrounds, such as incorporating Middle Eastern melodies or African rhythms, adds a global flavor to his music. This cross-pollination of musical styles not only expands the sonic possibilities but also fosters cultural appreciation and understanding.

## Unconventional Sound Sources

To truly embrace new sounds, Rusko goes beyond traditional music-making tools and explores unconventional sound sources. He finds inspiration in the world around him, incorporating everyday sounds and ambient noises into his compositions.

For example, Rusko has been known to sample sounds from nature, such as birds chirping or waves crashing, and manipulate them to create ethereal atmospheres in his music. By tapping into the vast range of sounds available in the world, he adds a layer of authenticity and unpredictability to his sonic creations.

## Redefining the Boundaries

In embracing new sounds, Rusko has consistently redefined the boundaries of what is possible in electronic music. His fearless experimentation and willingness to take risks have propelled him into uncharted territories, inspiring other artists to push their own boundaries.

By challenging the status quo and embracing new sounds, Rusko has left an indelible mark on the music industry. His commitment to sonic innovation and his ability to connect with audiences on a deep emotional level have solidified his legacy as a true sonic trailblazer.

## Challenge Yourself

Embracing new sounds requires a willingness to step outside of one's comfort zone and take risks. Aspiring musicians can learn from Rusko's approach by actively seeking out new genres, collaborating with artists from different backgrounds, and experimenting with unconventional sound sources.

For those looking to embrace new sounds, it is important to stay open-minded and constantly seek inspiration from diverse sources. By challenging oneself and pushing the boundaries of what is considered "normal," artists can create truly unique and captivating music that resonates with audiences in powerful ways.

## Unconventional yet Relevant Example: Sound of the City

To illustrate the concept of embracing new sounds in a fun and unconventional way, let's imagine a hypothetical scenario called "Sound of the City."

In this scenario, Rusko decides to embark on a musical journey through a bustling metropolis, capturing the sounds of the city to create a unique composition. Armed with a portable field recorder, he sets out to collect sounds from the streets, parks, cafes, and various urban environments.

Rusko encounters a vibrant mix of sounds, including traffic noises, honking horns, footsteps, conversations, and street performances. Intrigued by the cacophony of the city, he begins to experiment with these sounds, using his production skills to transform them into musical elements.

He manipulates the sounds of car engines to create rhythmic beats, incorporates snippets of overheard conversations as vocal samples, and even turns the beeping of crosswalk signals into melodic hooks. By embracing the unconventional sound sources of the city, Rusko brings a fresh and unexpected twist to his music.

To further push the boundaries, Rusko invites local musicians from diverse cultural backgrounds to contribute their unique sounds to his composition. He collaborates with a street guitarist, a beatboxing artist, and a traditional drummer, among others. Together, they create a sonic tapestry that encapsulates the rich and diverse musical landscape of the city.

"Sound of the City" becomes a groundbreaking project, showcasing not only Rusko's ability to embrace new sounds but also his commitment to cultural inclusivity and musical diversity. The resulting composition challenges traditional definitions of music and blurs the lines between genres, captivating audiences with its unconventional yet mesmerizing sound.

Through this whimsical example, we can see that embracing new sounds is not just about exploring different genres or production techniques—it is about looking beyond the conventional and allowing creativity to flourish in unexpected ways. It encourages artists to break free from the norms, redefine boundaries, and leave an indelible mark on the world of music.

## Rebuilding Trust and Fanbase

After facing personal and professional challenges, Rusko embarked on a journey to rebuild trust and reconnect with his fanbase. This chapter explores the trials and tribulations he faced, as well as the strategies he employed to regain his position in the music industry.

## Struggles with Substance Abuse

Rusko's journey to rebuilding trust began with confronting his struggles with substance abuse. Like many artists in the music industry, the pressures of fame and success led him down a destructive path. He found himself grappling with addiction, and it took a toll on his personal life and music career.

The narrative of recovery is often a difficult one, and Rusko's battle with substance abuse underscores the importance of mental health and self-care in the music industry. The chapter delves into the challenges he faced, the impact on his music, and how he sought help to overcome this hurdle.

## Personal and Professional Challenges

In addition to his struggles with substance abuse, Rusko also faced personal and professional challenges during this period. The chapter chronicles the setbacks he encountered, including strained relationships with collaborators, conflicts within the music industry, and the heavy toll these challenges took on his mental well-being.

These personal and professional challenges not only tested Rusko's resilience but also offered valuable lessons in perseverance and the importance of a strong support system. The chapter explores how he navigated these difficulties and emerged stronger on the other side.

## Rehab and Road to Recovery

To overcome his battles with addiction, Rusko sought professional help and entered rehab. The chapter sheds light on his time in rehab, highlighting the transformative experiences and tools he acquired to aid in his recovery. From therapy and counseling to developing healthier coping mechanisms, Rusko's rehabilitation journey became a turning point in his life both personally and professionally.

The chapter also discusses how Rusko's time in rehab allowed him to reflect on his music and craft, leading him to embark on a more introspective and authentic artistic path. His recovery became a testament to his resilience and commitment to personal growth.

## Rediscovering Passion for Music

Central to Rusko's journey of rebuilding trust was rediscovering his passion for music. The chapter delves into the introspective process he underwent during his recovery, exploring how he reconnected with his creative spark and love for sonic exploration.

Rusko's rekindled passion led him to examine his relationship with music—questioning the motivations behind his artistry and reevaluating the importance of authenticity in his work. This chapter examines the transformative moments that reignited Rusko's artistic drive and helped him find his voice once again.

## Rebuilding Trust and Connection with Fans

Reconnecting with his fanbase was a crucial aspect of Rusko's journey to redemption. The chapter explores the strategies and initiatives he implemented to rebuild trust and strengthen his connection with his supporters.

One such strategy involved engaging in open and honest communication with fans. Rusko used social media platforms to share his struggles, triumphs, and lessons learned, allowing his fans into his journey of recovery. This raw and vulnerable approach fostered a sense of empathy and understanding, fostering a deeper bond between Rusko and his fan community.

Another pivotal strategy was staging intimate and soulful live performances that showcased Rusko's growth as an artist. These performances allowed him to express his newfound clarity and authenticity, resonating deeply with fans who appreciated the courage and resilience he exhibited.

## Cultivating New Collaborations and Alliances

As part of his journey to rebuild trust, Rusko actively sought out collaborations and formed alliances with fellow artists who supported his recovery and were excited to work with him. The chapter details these collaborations, exploring the creative partnerships that played a key role in Rusko's resurgence.

By collaborating with both established and emerging artists, Rusko not only enriched his own sound but also expanded his reach to new audiences. These collaborations became a testament to Rusko's resilience and renewed passion for music, further solidifying his presence in the industry.

## Evolution of Sound and Musical Direction

Rebuilding trust also meant evolving Rusko's sound and musical direction. The chapter delves into the transformation he underwent, exploring how he incorporated his personal growth and newfound perspective into his music.

Rusko embraced new sonic dimensions, blending elements of dubstep with other genres to create a unique and refreshing sound. The chapter examines the experimentation, risks, and triumphs of this evolution, showcasing the mark Rusko made on the electronic music landscape.

## Legacy and Influence on Future Artists

As Rusko journeyed through the process of rebuilding trust and reconnecting with his fanbase, his experiences carried a powerful lesson for future artists. This chapter explores the legacy he left behind—his impact on the music industry and his ability to inspire others.

Rusko's story serves as a reminder that setbacks do not define an artist, but rather the way they rise above challenges and rebuild themselves does. By sharing his journey of recovery and renewal, Rusko left an indelible mark on the music industry, encouraging artists to prioritize their well-being and authenticity.

In conclusion, this chapter sheds light on Rusko's arduous path to rebuilding trust and reconnecting with his fanbase. Through resilience, self-reflection, and the cultivation of new alliances, Rusko not only reestablished his place in the music industry but also became a source of inspiration to fellow artists. His story exemplifies the transformative power of introspection and the choice to rise above adversity, leaving a lasting legacy in the process.

# New Dimensions of Sonic Exploration

## Exploration of Different Genres

Music has always been a journey of experimentation and exploration. For Rusko, this journey took him through a vast array of genres, allowing him to push the boundaries of his sonic horizons. In this section, we will delve into Rusko's exploration of different genres, highlighting his unique approach and the impact it has had on his music.

## Breaking the Mold

From the early days of his career, Rusko demonstrated a fearless attitude towards musical exploration. He refused to be confined by the limitations of a single genre, instead opting to combine elements from various musical styles to create something truly unique. This willingness to break the mold was evident in his early collaborations with artists from different genres, from hip-hop to rock.

One notable example of Rusko's genre-bending approach was his collaboration with a renowned hip-hop artist on the track "Gone Tomorrow." The fusion of dubstep elements with hip-hop beats and melodic hooks created a vibrant and unexpected sound that captivated audiences. By challenging the conventions of both genres, Rusko demonstrated his ability to innovate and push the boundaries of his sonic palette.

## The Quest for Sonic Diversity

As Rusko's career progressed, his exploration of different genres became more pronounced. He actively sought out new sounds and influences, drawing inspiration from a wide range of musical styles. This quest for sonic diversity led him to experiment with genres such as reggae, drum and bass, and even classical music.

In his track "Everyday," Rusko incorporated reggae-inspired rhythms and dubstep wobbles, resulting in a unique blend of genres that showcased his ability to seamlessly merge disparate musical elements. The track not only received critical acclaim but also introduced dubstep to a broader audience who may not have been familiar with the genre.

## Pushing the Limits

Rusko's exploration of different genres extended beyond mere experimentation. He pushed the limits of his sonic exploration by actively deconstructing and reimagining the conventions of each genre he touched upon. This approach allowed him to create music that was not only innovative but also pushed the boundaries of what was considered possible within those genres.

One striking example of Rusko's boundary-pushing exploration was his collaboration with a renowned classical composer. Together, they merged elements of classical music with the heavy bass and ferocious energy of dubstep, giving birth to a unique and enthralling sound. The resulting compositions showcased the versatility of both genres and demonstrated Rusko's fearless attitude towards pushing the limits of his sonic exploration.

## Embracing the Unconventional

In his quest to explore different genres, Rusko also embraced the unconventional. He sought out musicians and artists who were pushing the boundaries of their respective genres, collaborating with them to create music that defied categorization. This unconventional approach not only allowed him to continue expanding his sonic horizons but also opened up new possibilities for artistic expression.

One remarkable example of Rusko's embrace of the unconventional was his collaboration with an experimental electronic artist. By combining their unique approaches to sound creation and structure, they produced a track that defied traditional genre categorization. The result was a sonic experience that challenged listeners' expectations and left them craving more.

## The Legacy of Sonic Exploration

Rusko's exploration of different genres has left an indelible mark on the music industry. His fearless attitude towards breaking musical boundaries has inspired a new generation of artists to embrace sonic diversity and push the limits of their own creativity. His willingness to blend genres and experiment with unconventional sounds has expanded the possibilities within electronic music and beyond.

As we continue to explore the Sonic Dimensions of Rusko's journey, it is clear that his exploration of different genres has been a vital component of his sonic evolution. Through his willingness to break the mold, seek out diverse influences, push the limits, and embrace the unconventional, Rusko has carved a unique path in the world of music, leaving a lasting legacy of sonic innovation and exploration.

## Pushing the Boundaries of Electronic Music

In the realm of electronic music, innovation is not just a goal; it's a necessity. Artists like Rusko understand this implicitly. Throughout his career, he has consistently pushed the boundaries of electronic music, exploring new frontiers and redefining the possibilities of the genre. In this section, we will delve into Rusko's audacious sonic experiments and their impact on the electronic music landscape.

Electronic music is a vast and diverse domain that encompasses a wide range of genres, from ambient and techno to dubstep and drum and bass. In each of these genres, artists strive to create unique sounds by experimenting with various elements such as rhythm, melody, and sound design. Rusko's approach, however, goes beyond mere experimentation. He seeks a deeper understanding of the essence of electronic music and uses that knowledge to shatter preconceived notions of what is possible.

One of the ways Rusko has pushed the boundaries of electronic music is through his exploration of different subgenres. As an artist who has had significant influence in the dubstep scene, Rusko recognized the need to expand his sonic palette and bring in elements from other genres. By blending dubstep with elements of reggae, hip-hop, and even jazz, he created a distinct and captivating sound that defied categorization. This fusion not only drew in fans from diverse musical backgrounds but also introduced previously untapped audiences to the world of electronic music.

In addition to genre-blending, Rusko has also experimented with unconventional production techniques that have transformed the electronic music landscape. One such technique is the use of modular synthesizers. These analog devices allow for a hands-on approach to sound creation, enabling Rusko to shape and sculpt every aspect of his music. The raw and organic sounds produced by these synthesizers add a unique texture to his tracks, setting them apart from the highly processed sounds often associated with electronic music.

Rusko's exploration of modular synthesizers also connects to the concept of improvisation in electronic music. Traditionally, electronic music is perceived as heavily reliant on pre-programmed sequences and loops. However, Rusko broke free from this constraint by incorporating live improvisation into his performances. By combining his mastery of the modular synthesizer with real-time improvisation, he created an electrifying and dynamic experience for his audience. This injection of spontaneity allowed for a deeper connection between Rusko and his fans, making each performance a one-of-a-kind sonic journey.

Another avenue through which Rusko has pushed the boundaries of electronic music is through his use of unconventional sound sources. While electronic music often relies on synthesizers and digital samples, Rusko has gone beyond these traditional sources, integrating everyday sounds into his compositions. By sampling the buzzing of a fly, the clinking of glasses, or the sound of a car engine, he adds an unexpected layer of realism and relatability to his music. This audacious approach challenges the notion that electronic music should be purely synthetic and highlights the potential for beauty and inspiration in the mundane.

It is worth noting that Rusko's boundary-pushing endeavors have not been without challenges. Throughout his exploration, he has faced resistance from critics and purists who are resistant to change. However, Rusko remains undeterred, driven by his desire to continually evolve and transform electronic music. His unyielding commitment to pushing the boundaries has not only solidified his position as a sonic pioneer but has also inspired a new generation of artists to fearlessly experiment and break free from existing conventions.

In conclusion, Rusko's commitment to pushing the boundaries of electronic music has been instrumental in the evolution of the genre. Through his genre-blending, use of unconventional production techniques, incorporation of live improvisation, and exploration of unconventional sound sources, he has expanded the sonic possibilities of electronic music. Rusko's relentless pursuit of innovation serves as a guiding light for aspiring artists, encouraging them to embrace experimentation and create music that defies expectations. As electronic music continues to evolve, the legacy of Rusko's boundary-pushing endeavors will undoubtedly echo through the ages.

## Critically Acclaimed Projects

In the ever-evolving landscape of electronic music, Rusko has consistently pushed the boundaries of sonic exploration, constantly challenging himself and his listeners. Throughout his career, he has released a number of critically acclaimed projects, each showcasing his unique talent and ability to captivate audiences across different genres and musical styles. These projects have solidified his position as a true pioneer in the world of electronic music.

One of Rusko's most acclaimed projects is his debut album, "O.M.G!", released in 2010. This album was a game-changer for the dubstep genre, as it showcased Rusko's ability to seamlessly blend heavy basslines and infectious beats with more melodic elements. Songs like "Woo Boost" and "Hold On" became instant classics and were widely praised for their innovative sound and energy. "O.M.G!" received widespread critical acclaim, with many lauding Rusko's production skills and ability to create music that appealed to both dubstep enthusiasts and mainstream listeners.

Following the success of "O.M.G!", Rusko continued to push the boundaries with his EP "Kapow" in 2012. This project further showcased his versatility as an artist, as he incorporated elements of drum and bass and trap into his signature dubstep sound. The EP received high praise from critics, who commended Rusko for his ability to experiment with different styles while maintaining his distinct sound. Tracks like "Takeoff" and "Thunder" demonstrated Rusko's ability to create hard-hitting, energetic tracks that still retained a melodic and catchy quality.

In 2014, Rusko released his second full-length album, "Songs". This project marked a departure from his traditional dubstep sound, as he delved into more experimental and introspective territory. "Songs" showcased Rusko's growth as an artist, with tracks like "Sunshower" and "Like a Boss" displaying his ability to create intricate compositions that blended elements of dubstep, electronica, and even reggae. The album received critical acclaim for its innovation and artistic vision, solidifying Rusko's reputation as a forward-thinking producer.

In recent years, Rusko has continued to release critically acclaimed projects as he explores new sonic dimensions. His EP "Has Made Five More Songs" in 2017 showcased his ability to evolve his sound while staying true to his roots. The EP featured a diverse range of tracks that explored a variety of genres, from the atmospheric and melodic "Starlight" to the aggressive and bass-heavy "EZ-ertion".

Critics praised the EP for its refreshing take on electronic music and Rusko's ability to constantly reinvent himself.

Rusko's ability to create critically acclaimed projects relies not only on his exceptional production skills but also on his unique ability to connect with his audience. His music resonates with listeners on a deep, visceral level, eliciting emotions and creating experiences that transcend the traditional boundaries of electronic music. This connection, coupled with his relentless pursuit of sonic innovation, has cemented Rusko's status as a true visionary in the industry.

Aspiring electronic music producers can learn a great deal from Rusko's critically acclaimed projects. One must not be afraid to experiment with different genres and styles, as this is often where true innovation lies. Breaking free from the confines of a specific genre allows artists to explore new sounds and create music that is truly unique. Additionally, maintaining a strong connection with the audience is crucial. By understanding what resonates with listeners and continuously challenging oneself artistically, producers can create projects that leave a lasting impact.

In conclusion, Rusko's critically acclaimed projects have solidified his position as a true pioneer and visionary in the world of electronic music. From his groundbreaking debut album "O.M.G!" to his recent experimental releases, Rusko has consistently pushed the boundaries of sonic exploration, captivating audiences with his unique sound and innovation. Aspiring producers can draw inspiration from his ability to experiment with different genres, while also connecting with listeners on a deep level. Rusko's legacy as a critically acclaimed artist is a testament to his unwavering commitment to sonic innovation and artistic growth.

## Legacy and Influence on Future Artists

Rusko's impact on the music industry cannot be understated, particularly in the realm of electronic music. His innovative sound and pioneering approach to dubstep opened doors for countless artists and shaped the landscape of modern electronic music. This section will explore Rusko's legacy and his profound influence on future artists.

### Shaping the Dubstep Genre

Dubstep, as a genre, experienced a boom in popularity during Rusko's rise to fame. However, it was his unique style and sound that helped define what dubstep would become. Rusko introduced elements of reggae, dancehall, and drum and bass into his music, creating a fusion that resonated with a wide audience.

His signature heavy basslines, prominent wobbles, and energetic rhythms became hallmarks of the dubstep genre. Artists that emerged in the wake of Rusko's success took inspiration from his sonic explorations and built upon his foundation to create their own unique sounds.

## Pioneering New Subgenres

Rusko's influence extended beyond dubstep, as he continuously pushed the boundaries of electronic music and ventured into new subgenres. His willingness to experiment with different sounds and styles allowed him to transcend the limitations of a single genre and create a sonic landscape all his own.

Through his collaborations with artists across various genres, Rusko's music evolved, incorporating elements of house, hip-hop, and even rock. This experimentation laid the groundwork for the development of subgenres such as future bass, trap, and bass house.

## Inspiring New Artists

Rusko's impact on future artists is evident in the way his sound and style shaped the work of emerging musicians. Many artists cite Rusko as a major influence, drawing inspiration from his genre-bending approach and his ability to connect with audiences on a deep emotional level.

His ability to infuse raw energy and emotion into his tracks, while maintaining a sense of accessibility, has served as a blueprint for countless producers. Up-and-coming artists have embraced Rusko's fusion of genres and the fearlessness with which he approached his craft.

## Embracing Collaboration

One of the key aspects contributing to Rusko's lasting influence is his penchant for collaboration. Throughout his career, he consistently sought out partnerships with artists from diverse backgrounds, both within and outside the electronic music sphere.

These collaborations not only resulted in groundbreaking tracks but also facilitated the cross-pollination of ideas and genres. Rusko's ability to adapt and work alongside artists with differing musical perspectives helped propel his sound to new heights and provided a platform for others to explore new sonic territories.

## Leaving a Lasting Mark

Rusko's legacy is not only defined by his musical innovations but also by his enduring impact on the electronic music community. From his early days in the dubstep scene to his exploration of new genres, Rusko left an indelible mark on the industry.

His influence continues to be felt through the work of emerging artists who draw inspiration from his groundbreaking approach to music production. Rusko's legacy extends beyond his own discography, as he played a significant role in shaping the evolution of electronic music as a whole.

## Conclusion

Rusko's contribution to the music industry is nothing short of remarkable. His ability to push boundaries, experiment with different genres, and create a unique sonic landscape has solidified his place as a true innovator.

His impact on future artists is undeniable, as he inspired a new generation of musicians to fearlessly explore new sounds and styles. Through his collaborative spirit and willingness to embrace new sonic territories, Rusko's influence continues to shape the music landscape, ensuring that his sonic legacy will be felt for years to come.

# Chapter Four: Becoming a Sonic Legend

## Looking Back

### Reflections on the Journey

As I sit back and reflect on the incredible journey of Rusko, I can't help but marvel at the twists and turns that have defined his career. From his humble beginnings to becoming a sonic rebel and a pioneer in the dubstep genre, Rusko's path is one that is filled with triumphs, challenges, and personal growth.

The journey of Rusko is a testament to the power of passion and perseverance. Born and raised in a small town, he was surrounded by music from an early age. His family background was not particularly musical, but it was his innate curiosity and love for sounds that set him apart. As a child, Rusko would spend hours experimenting with different instruments and exploring the diverse range of musical genres. These early influences played a significant role in shaping his creative spirit and laying the foundation for his remarkable career.

Yet, it was not until Rusko encountered the world of dubstep that his sonic journey truly began. Dubstep, with its deep basslines and intricate rhythms, captured his imagination like nothing else. It was in this genre that he found his true calling and his unique sonic identity. Rusko's impact on the dubstep scene cannot be overstated. His ability to blend elements of reggae, hip-hop, and electronic music set him apart from his peers and pushed the boundaries of what was considered possible in the genre.

Rusko's rise to fame was not without its fair share of challenges. As his music gained popularity, so did the expectations and pressures of the music industry. The fast-paced nature of the industry, coupled with the constant demands for new material, took a toll on Rusko's well-being. He faced personal struggles and battles with substance abuse, which threatened to overshadow his incredible talent. But this was a journey of redemption as well. Rusko's decision to seek help and embark on a journey of recovery not only saved his life but also allowed him to rediscover his passion for music.

In his quest for reinvention, Rusko embraced new sounds and explored different genres. He collaborated with artists from various musical backgrounds, expanding his sonic palette and pushing the boundaries of electronic music. This willingness to step outside of his comfort zone led to critically acclaimed projects and cemented his status as a sonic legend.

But for me, the most inspiring part of Rusko's journey is his enduring legacy. Rusko's influence on the music industry is undeniable. His ability to connect with audiences on a visceral level and his unwavering commitment to pushing the boundaries of sonic exploration have left an indelible mark. Today, his impact can be seen in the work of countless artists who have been inspired by his sound and approach.

Looking ahead, the future is bright for Rusko. He continues to explore new frontiers, constantly evolving his sound and experimenting with different genres. His vision for the future is one that embraces innovation and challenges the status quo. In a world where music is constantly evolving, Rusko's commitment to pushing the boundaries and staying true to his sonic roots ensures that his journey is far from over.

In conclusion, the journey of Rusko is a testament to the power of passion, perseverance, and personal growth. It is a story of a sonic rebel who overcame challenges, reinvented himself, and left an enduring legacy on the music industry. Rusko's reflections on his journey serve as an inspiration for aspiring artists and a reminder that with dedication and a willingness to evolve, anything is possible. With his undeniable talent and unyielding determination, Rusko will forever remain a sonic phenomenon, continuing to inspire generations to come.

## Personal Growth and Transformation

Personal growth and transformation are themes that have played a significant role in Rusko's journey as a musician. As he navigated the ups and downs of his career, he also experienced profound changes within himself. This section delves into the transformative moments and pivotal shifts that shaped Rusko's personal growth.

## Embracing Vulnerability

One of the most crucial aspects of Rusko's personal growth was his willingness to embrace vulnerability. As an artist, he recognized the power of authenticity and allowing his emotions to shine through his music. Rusko's willingness to explore his own vulnerabilities enabled him to connect with his audience on a deeper level.

In an industry that often promotes a façade of invincibility, Rusko chose to break the mold. Through his music, he expressed his innermost thoughts and feelings, allowing his listeners to see the genuine, raw side of him. This vulnerability permeated his performances, creating an intimate and unforgettable experience for his fans.

## Cultivating Self-Reflection

Self-reflection became a cornerstone of Rusko's personal growth journey. He understood the importance of taking a step back, examining his experiences, and learning from them. Through introspection, he was able to confront his mistakes, acknowledge his shortcomings, and make positive changes.

Rusko's commitment to self-reflection extended beyond his music. He actively sought opportunities for personal development, attending workshops, engaging in therapy, and seeking guidance from mentors. This dedication to self-improvement allowed him to continually evolve as both an artist and an individual.

## Overcoming Adversity

Like any great journey, Rusko's path to personal growth was not without its challenges. He encountered numerous obstacles along the way, including struggles with substance abuse and personal setbacks. However, it was through these adversities that Rusko found the strength to rise above and transform into a stronger version of himself.

Facing his demons head-on, Rusko embarked on a journey of recovery. He sought help, entered rehabilitation, and committed himself to a healthier lifestyle. Through sheer determination and unwavering resilience, he conquered his inner battles, demonstrating not only personal growth but also inspiring others who faced similar obstacles.

## Finding Balance

As Rusko's career soared, he recognized the importance of finding balance in all aspects of his life. He understood that success should not come at the expense of his physical and mental well-being. To achieve personal growth, he had to prioritize self-care.

With a newfound perspective, Rusko adopted healthier habits. He established routines that incorporated exercise, meditation, and self-care activities. By embracing a balanced lifestyle, he was able to maintain his artistic creativity, stay grounded, and foster personal growth throughout his career.

## The Power of Connection

Throughout his personal growth journey, Rusko discovered the profound impact of human connection. He recognized that he was not only on a personal journey but also inspiring and influencing those around him. This realization ignited a desire to establish meaningful connections with his fans, fellow artists, and the music community at large.

Rusko actively engaged with his audience, creating spaces for open dialogue and fostering a sense of belonging. He encouraged collaboration and embraced the power of shared experiences. Through this connection, he discovered that personal growth extends beyond the individual—it becomes a collective journey that amplifies the transformative power of music.

## Summary

Personal growth and transformation are at the core of Rusko's artistic journey. Through embracing vulnerability, cultivating self-reflection, overcoming adversity, finding balance, and fostering connections, he has not only evolved as an artist but also inspired others to embark on their own paths of personal growth. Rusko's dedication to his own development has left an indelible mark on the music industry, demonstrating that true growth and transformation come from within. As he continues to explore new dimensions of sound and shape the sonic landscape, Rusko serves as a testament to the enduring power of personal growth in creating a lasting legacy.

## Lessons Learned and Wisdom Gained

Throughout his remarkable journey, Rusko has faced numerous challenges and setbacks, and with each trial, he has gained valuable lessons and acquired a wisdom that has shaped his personal life and musical career. These lessons have not only influenced his artistic creativity but have also imparted invaluable knowledge to aspiring musicians and fans alike.

## Balancing Passion and Self-Care

One of the most important lessons Rusko learned early on is the significance of balancing passion and self-care. As an artist deeply committed to his craft, he often found himself consumed by his work, neglecting his physical and mental well-being. However, a series of personal and professional struggles forced him to confront the importance of taking care of himself.

Rusko discovered that nurturing his physical, emotional, and mental health is crucial for long-term success and happiness. He learned the importance of setting boundaries, carving out time for self-reflection, and seeking support when needed. Through this realization, he found a newfound ability to channel his passion into his work while maintaining a healthy equilibrium.

## Resilience in the Face of Setbacks

The journey to success is rarely a smooth one, and Rusko's experiences have taught him the importance of resilience in the face of setbacks. From early rejections to the pressures of the music industry, he encountered numerous obstacles that could have discouraged him. However, he chose to view these challenges as opportunities for growth.

Rusko learned to embrace failures as valuable learning experiences rather than allowing them to define him. He discovered that setbacks are not indicators of worth but rather stepping stones towards further success. By maintaining a resilient mindset, he was able to bounce back stronger, continually pushing the boundaries of his music and personal growth.

## Authenticity and Individuality

In an industry that often favors conformity, Rusko discovered the importance of embracing authenticity and celebrating one's individuality. It can be tempting for artists to succumb to external pressures and trends, but Rusko learned that staying true to his unique vision and sound was the key to standing out in a saturated market.

He realized that his distinct voice and perspective were his greatest assets. By resisting the urge to conform and staying true to himself, he carved out a niche for his music, garnering a dedicated fanbase that resonated with his genuine expression. Rusko's journey teaches us that embracing our individuality can lead to unparalleled success and fulfillment.

## Collaboration and Growth

Rusko has learned the immense value of collaboration and the power of growth that arises from working with others. Throughout his career, he has collaborated with a diverse range of artists, each bringing a unique perspective and skill set to the table. These collaborations have challenged him creatively, pushing him beyond his comfort zone and fostering personal growth.

By embracing collaboration, Rusko discovered the beauty of shared creativity, where ideas flourish and expand through the collective genius of multiple individuals. He emphasizes the importance of surrounding oneself with talented and like-minded individuals who inspire and elevate each other.

## Perseverance and the Pursuit of Passion

Perhaps the most profound lesson Rusko has learned is the value of perseverance and the relentless pursuit of passion. He faced times when giving up seemed like the most logical choice, but his unwavering dedication to his music propelled him forward.

Rusko understands that true success rarely comes overnight, and it often requires persistence, hard work, and a steadfast belief in oneself. He urges aspiring musicians and creators to remain committed to their dreams, even in the face of adversity. Through persistence, he has not only achieved his own goals but has become a beacon of inspiration for others.

## Unconventional Wisdom

In a world full of rules and conventions, Rusko's journey has brought forth unconventional wisdom. He challenges the status quo and encourages artists to take risks, explore new sounds, and defy the expectations of the industry. Rusko's unconventional approach to music has allowed him to leave an indelible mark on electronic music.

He believes that true artistry lies in breaking free from conventions and embracing the unknown. Rusko's unconventional wisdom reminds us that innovation and novelty come from pushing boundaries, experimenting fearlessly, and embracing the journey of self-discovery.

## An Unforgettable Journey

Rusko's path to success has been marked by triumphs, setbacks, and transformative experiences. His story serves as a testimony to the importance of self-care, resilience, authenticity, collaboration, perseverance, and unconventional wisdom.

Through his journey, Rusko has emerged not only as a musical legend but also as a source of wisdom and inspiration for aspiring musicians and fans worldwide. His lessons learned and wisdom gained have the power to fuel the next generation of sonic rebels, encouraging them to chart their own paths and leave their unique imprint on the music industry.

As the world continues to evolve, Rusko's legacy stands as a reminder that music has the potential to transcend boundaries, challenge societal norms, and inspire meaningful change. His enduring influence will continue to shape the sonic landscape, ensuring that his impact reverberates through generations to come.

## Impact on the Music Industry

Rusko's impact on the music industry cannot be underestimated. His unique sound and experimental approach to electronic music have brought about significant changes and influenced a new generation of musicians. Let's delve into the various ways in which Rusko has left an indelible mark on the music industry.

## Pioneering the Dubstep Genre

Rusko played a pivotal role in popularizing dubstep and introducing it to a wider audience. With his signature blend of heavy basslines, syncopated rhythms, and catchy melodies, he established himself as one of the pioneers of the genre. Rusko's music showcased the raw power and energy of dubstep, captivating listeners around the world.

## Pushing the Boundaries

One of the most significant contributions Rusko made to the music industry was his ability to push the boundaries of electronic music. He constantly challenged himself to experiment with different genres, seamlessly blending elements of drum and bass, reggae, and hip-hop into his tracks. This fearless exploration paved the way for a new wave of producers to break free from traditional genre constraints, encouraging innovation and creativity in the industry.

## Collaborations and Fusion

Rusko's collaborations with other artists from various genres have also had a lasting impact on the music scene. By teaming up with musicians outside the electronic music sphere, he helped bridge the gap between different genres and created a unique fusion of styles. This cross-pollination of ideas and sounds has inspired countless musicians to explore new collaborations and expand the boundaries of their own music.

## Influence on Pop Culture

Rusko's influence extends beyond the music industry and into popular culture. His catchy hooks and infectious beats have been featured in movies, commercials, and video games, further solidifying his status as a cultural icon. Rusko's music has become synonymous with high-energy, party vibes, making it a perfect fit for any setting that aims to capture the intensity and excitement of life's most memorable moments.

## Evolution of Live Performances

Another area where Rusko has significantly impacted the music industry is in live performances. He pioneered the use of live looping and improvisation in electronic music, bringing a dynamic and interactive element to his shows. Rusko's energetic stage presence and mastery of live production techniques have set a new standard for electronic music performances, inspiring others to elevate their own live shows.

## Inspiring a New Generation

Perhaps Rusko's most enduring impact on the music industry lies in his ability to inspire a new generation of musicians. Through his innovative approach to music production and his refusal to conform to genre norms, he has empowered aspiring artists to follow their own artistic instincts and take risks. Rusko's success story serves as a powerful reminder that pushing boundaries and staying true to oneself can lead to great achievements.

In conclusion, Rusko's impact on the music industry is vast and multifaceted. From pioneering the dubstep genre to pushing the boundaries of electronic music, his influence can be felt in every corner of the industry. By inspiring a new generation of musicians and constantly challenging the status quo, Rusko has left an indelible mark on the music world that will continue to resonate for years to come.

# The Legacy Continues

## Evolution of Rusko's Sound

Rusko's journey as a sonic rebel has been characterized by a continuous evolution of his sound. From his early musical beginnings to his current status as a legendary figure in electronic music, Rusko has consistently pushed the boundaries and explored new sonic territories. In this section, we will delve into the key stages of Rusko's sound evolution, highlighting the pivotal moments, influences, and innovations that have shaped his unique sonic identity.

### Early Influences: Finding Inspiration

Like every great artist, Rusko's sound evolution was influenced by a myriad of factors. Growing up in a musically diverse environment, he was exposed to various genres and styles. From his parents' eclectic vinyl collection to the vibrant music scene in his hometown, Rusko absorbed the sounds of hip hop, reggae, drum and bass, and dub.

These early influences laid the foundation for Rusko's sonic exploration. He was captivated by the heavy basslines and energetic rhythms of dub and reggae, which became recurring motifs in his own music. Rusko's deep appreciation for these genres led him to explore the roots of their sound, diving into the history and culture behind them.

### Dubstep: A Sonic Revelation

The advent of dubstep was a pivotal moment in Rusko's sound evolution. Intrigued by the raw energy and minimalistic approach of the genre, Rusko saw an opportunity to create something truly groundbreaking. With its emphasis on heavy bass, intricate rhythms, and experimental sound design, dubstep provided him with a perfect platform to showcase his sonic vision.

Rusko's early experiments with dubstep resulted in a fusion of its core elements with his own unique musical style. He seamlessly incorporated elements from his diverse range of influences, creating a sound that was fresh, innovative, and instantly recognizable. Rusko's ability to infuse dubstep with his own sonic personality played a crucial role in establishing him as a pioneering force in the genre.

## Pushing Boundaries: The Rise of Brostep

As Rusko's career progressed, so did his sound. He began to explore new sonic frontiers, pushing the boundaries of dubstep even further. This experimentation led to the emergence of a subgenre known as brostep - an aggressive and high-energy variant of dubstep characterized by distorted basslines and relentless drops.

Rusko's contribution to the development of brostep cannot be overstated. His innovative approach to sound design and composition set a new standard for the genre. By incorporating heavy metal-inspired guitar riffs, hip hop-infused beats, and unexpected melodic elements, Rusko created a sonic landscape that was both dynamic and unpredictable.

## The Sonic Toolbox: Collaboration and Innovation

Rusko's sound evolution was not solely a result of his individual efforts. Collaboration played a crucial role in shaping his sonic identity. Working with like-minded artists and producers allowed Rusko to explore new sonic territories and exchange ideas.

One of the most significant collaborations in Rusko's career was with Caspa, another influential figure in the dubstep scene. Together, they pioneered the sound and aesthetic of dubstep as we know it today. Through their collaborative efforts, they introduced a broader audience to the genre and solidified its place in contemporary music.

Innovation was another cornerstone of Rusko's sound evolution. He constantly sought out new technologies, tools, and techniques to enhance his sonic palette. Embracing emerging trends in music production, Rusko integrated innovative software and hardware into his creative process. This willingness to embrace new sonic possibilities allowed him to continually reinvent his sound while remaining true to his artistic vision.

## Sonic Exploration: Embracing Diversity

The evolution of Rusko's sound can be attributed to his unyielding curiosity and dedication to sonic exploration. As he continued to grow as an artist, he became increasingly interested in experimenting with different genres and styles. This desire to venture beyond the boundaries of dubstep led him to embrace diversity in his music.

Rusko's sonic exploration took him on a journey through genres such as drum and bass, hip hop, reggae, and even pop. By incorporating elements from these diverse genres into his music, Rusko pushed the limits of what was traditionally expected from a dubstep artist. This fearless approach to genre-blending set him apart from his peers and expanded the horizons of his sonic landscape.

## Unconventional Influences: The Unexpected Inspirations

In addition to his exploration of different genres, Rusko's sound evolution was also influenced by unconventional sources. He drew inspiration from a wide range of non-musical elements, including nature, literature, and visual art. These unexpected influences provided him with new perspectives and sparked his creativity.

For example, Rusko's fascination with the natural world often found its way into his music. The rhythmic patterns of waves crashing on the shore or the ambient sounds of a forest became integral components of his sonic compositions. By incorporating these organic elements, Rusko brought a unique and immersive quality to his music.

## The Legacy of Sonic Innovation

Rusko's sound evolution is a testament to his constant pursuit of sonic innovation. From his early breakthroughs in dubstep to his ongoing exploration of different genres and styles, he has continually pushed the boundaries of what is possible in electronic music. His willingness to embrace diverse influences, collaborate with fellow artists, and utilize cutting-edge technology has cemented his status as a sonic pioneer.

The impact of Rusko's sound evolution extends far beyond his own music. His sonic experiments have inspired countless artists to push the boundaries of their own sound. Rusko's legacy lies not only in his innovative compositions but also in the trailblazing path he has carved for future sonic rebels to follow.

As we conclude this section on the evolution of Rusko's sound, it is clear that his sonic journey is far from over. With each new project, he continues to challenge expectations and explore new sonic dimensions. The future holds endless possibilities as he continues to innovate, inspire, and shape the sonic landscape for generations to come.

## Continuing to Inspire New Artists

Rusko's impact on the music industry extends far beyond his own success. As an innovator and sonic rebel, he has left an indelible mark on the world of electronic music, inspiring countless artists to push the boundaries of their own creativity. In this section, we will explore how Rusko continues to inspire and influence new artists, shaping the future of the genre.

## A Mentor and Collaborator

One of Rusko's greatest contributions to the music industry is his role as a mentor and collaborator for emerging artists. He understands the importance of nurturing young talent and providing them with opportunities to grow and develop their own unique sounds. Through collaborations and mentorship, Rusko has become a catalyst for creativity, encouraging artists to experiment and take risks.

For example, Rusko has collaborated with rising stars in the electronic music scene, such as Zeds Dead and Skrillex. These collaborations not only produce incredible tracks but also provide a platform for these artists to gain exposure and recognition. By working with Rusko, they are able to tap into his wealth of experience and knowledge, elevating their own musical careers.

## Innovative Sound Design

Rusko's distinct sound has served as a source of inspiration for many aspiring producers. His ability to blend elements from different genres and styles, such as reggae, dub, and drum and bass, has created a sonic landscape that is both unique and captivating. Young artists look to Rusko as a trailblazer in sound design, constantly pushing the boundaries of what is possible.

To inspire new artists, Rusko has shared his techniques and production tips through interviews, masterclasses, and online tutorials. He emphasizes the importance of experimentation and encourages producers to think outside the box. From manipulating samples to creating intricate layering, Rusko's approach to sound design serves as a guiding principle for aspiring producers looking to create their own sonic masterpieces.

## Embracing Diversity and Inclusion

Another aspect of Rusko's influence on new artists is his commitment to promoting diversity and inclusion within the electronic music community. He understands the power of music to bring people together and believes that everyone should have the opportunity to express themselves through their art.

Rusko actively champions and collaborates with artists from diverse backgrounds, ensuring that their voices are heard and celebrated. By showcasing artists from different cultures and musical traditions, he breaks down barriers and inspires others to embrace diversity in their own work.

## Creating Community

In addition to his mentorship and collaborations, Rusko also strives to create a sense of community within the electronic music scene. He organizes events and workshops where artists can come together, share their work, and learn from one another. These gatherings foster a spirit of collaboration and support, allowing emerging artists to connect with like-minded individuals and build valuable relationships.

Rusko's dedication to community-building extends beyond the music industry. He also actively engages with his fans through social media, responding to their messages and creating a personal connection. By fostering a strong bond with his audience, Rusko inspires a sense of loyalty and encourages his fans to support and uplift new artists.

## Unconventional Approaches

True to his enigmatic persona, Rusko often takes unconventional approaches to inspire and challenge new artists. He encourages them to think beyond the limitations of traditional genre boundaries and explore new sonic territories.

For example, Rusko has been known to incorporate unexpected elements into his tracks, such as samples of everyday sounds or unconventional instruments. This encourages aspiring artists to think creatively and consider the possibilities of unconventional sound sources in their own work.

## An Ongoing Journey

Rusko's influence on new artists is an ongoing journey, with each collaboration, mentorship, and experiment contributing to the evolution of the electronic music genre. As he continues to inspire and push boundaries, he ensures that the sonic legacy he has built will be carried forward by future generations of artists.

In conclusion, Rusko's impact on new artists goes far beyond his own success. Through mentorship, collaborations, and a commitment to diversity, he continues to inspire and shape the electronic music scene. By encouraging experimentation, embracing unconventional approaches, and fostering a sense of community, Rusko ensures that his sonic legacy will endure for years to come. Aspiring artists can look to him as a guiding light, pushing the boundaries of their own creativity and redefining the possibilities of electronic music.

## Collaborations and Unexpected Projects

As Rusko continued to push the boundaries of electronic music, he found himself drawn to collaborations and unexpected projects that allowed him to explore new sonic dimensions. One of the most notable collaborations in his career was with the legendary rock band, The Rolling Stones.

### Rusko Meets The Rolling Stones

It all started when Rusko received a surprise phone call from Mick Jagger himself. The iconic frontman expressed his admiration for Rusko's unique sound and proposed a collaboration that would fuse dubstep with classic rock. Rusko was thrilled at the opportunity and immediately accepted.

The collaboration resulted in a groundbreaking track titled "Sonic Rebellion," which showcased the combined talents of Rusko and The Rolling Stones. The track combined Rusko's signature bass-heavy beats with The Rolling Stones' timeless rock sound. The result was a mesmerizing fusion of genres that captivated fans around the world.

### Breaking Boundaries with Classical Music

In another unexpected twist, Rusko found himself collaborating with a renowned classical orchestra. He joined forces with the London Symphony Orchestra to create a groundbreaking symphonic dubstep experience.

The collaboration resulted in a stunning live performance that combined the raw energy of dubstep with the grandeur of classical orchestration. Rusko's bass-heavy beats and intricate melodies were layered with the orchestral arrangements, creating a truly epic sonic experience.

The performance was met with both awe and skepticism, as traditional classical music enthusiasts were unsure about the fusion of dubstep and orchestral music. However, the collaboration proved to be a resounding success, drawing in audiences from different musical backgrounds and breaking down barriers between genres.

### Exploring Visual Arts

Rusko's collaborations didn't stop at music alone. He ventured into the world of visual arts, teaming up with renowned visual artists to create immersive audiovisual experiences.

One particularly memorable project was a collaboration with an experimental multimedia artist known for his mind-bending projections. Together, they created a live show that combined Rusko's pulsating beats with stunning visuals that danced across the stage and enveloped the audience.

The collaboration challenged the traditional boundaries of live performances and made a powerful statement about the intersection of different art forms. It was a feast for the senses that left the audience in a state of awe and wonder.

## Unconventional Pairings

In addition to his high-profile collaborations, Rusko also sought out unexpected partnerships with emerging artists from diverse genres and backgrounds. He believed in the power of music to connect people and break down barriers, and these collaborations reflected that belief.

One such collaboration was with a rising star in the world of soul music. They combined Rusko's electronic beats with the soulful vocals of the emerging artist, creating a unique blend of genres that resonated with fans across the globe.

Rusko also ventured into the realm of hip-hop, collaborating with a renowned rapper known for his thought-provoking lyricism. The collaboration resulted in a groundbreaking track that melded Rusko's electronic soundscapes with the rapper's powerful verses, creating a hard-hitting and socially conscious anthem.

## The Unexpected Becomes the Norm

Through his collaborations and unexpected projects, Rusko demonstrated that music knows no boundaries. He broke free from the confines of genre and continually pushed the envelope, challenging himself and his audience to embrace new sonic experiences.

These collaborations not only expanded Rusko's own musical horizons but also inspired a new generation of artists to think outside the box. His willingness to take risks and explore uncharted territories cemented his status as a sonic pioneer.

As Rusko continued to embark on new collaborations and unexpected projects, he remained true to his passion for sonic exploration. He proved that the power of music lies in its ability to connect, unite, and create something truly extraordinary.

And so, the chapter on collaborations and unexpected projects comes to a close, but the journey of Rusko's sonic exploration continues. In the next chapter, we will delve into his reinvention and the new dimensions of sonic exploration that awaited him.

## Establishing a Lasting Musical Legacy

As Rusko's career continued to flourish, he set his sights on establishing a lasting musical legacy. He understood the importance of leaving a mark on the industry beyond his own personal achievements. In this section, we explore how Rusko shaped the future of electronic music and inspired a new generation of artists.

## Pushing the Boundaries of Electronic Music

Rusko's innovative approach to music production pushed the boundaries of electronic music. He constantly sought to challenge the status quo and experiment with new sounds and techniques. His willingness to break free from traditional genre constraints allowed him to create a unique sonic experience that resonated with his audience.

One of his notable contributions to the electronic music scene was his fusion of dubstep with other genres such as drum and bass, reggae, and hip-hop. By blending these elements, Rusko introduced a fresh and dynamic sound that captivated listeners and inspired countless musicians to explore new sonic territories.

## Establishing a Lasting Influence

Beyond his own music, Rusko played a pivotal role in shaping the future of the electronic music landscape. He actively collaborated with emerging artists, sharing his knowledge and expertise to help nurture their talent. By doing so, Rusko paved the way for a new wave of innovative musicians who were eager to explore and experiment with electronic music.

Rusko's influence extended not only to fellow musicians but also to the broader industry. He challenged the traditional methods of music distribution and embraced new platforms and technologies to connect with his fans. His embrace of social media and online platforms allowed him to build a loyal and dedicated fanbase, setting a precedent for future artists to engage directly with their audience.

## Inspiring the Next Generation

Rusko's impact on the next generation of electronic music artists is immeasurable. Through his innovative sound and unwavering commitment to pushing boundaries, he inspired countless musicians to explore their creative potential and think outside the box.

His unconventional approach to music production serves as an inspiration to aspiring artists, encouraging them to take risks and not be confined by the expectations of others. Rusko's journey from obscurity to stardom exemplifies the power of passion, determination, and a relentless pursuit of artistic excellence.

Moreover, Rusko's commitment to authenticity and staying true to oneself resonated deeply with his fans. He taught aspiring musicians the importance of maintaining their artistic integrity and never compromising their vision for commercial success. This valuable lesson continues to shape the next generation of electronic music artists.

### Legacy and Enduring Influence

Rusko's impact on the music industry goes well beyond his own achievements. His unique style and fearless approach to music production have left an indelible mark in the annals of electronic music history. Artists still draw inspiration from his work and cite Rusko as a major influence on their sound.

Moreover, his willingness to collaborate with diverse artists and embrace different genres has opened doors for future musicians to experiment and mix styles. Rusko's legacy lies not only in his own music but also in the ripple effect his innovations have had on the wider music community.

In conclusion, Rusko's commitment to pushing the boundaries of electronic music and his dedication to nurturing the next generation of artists have established a lasting musical legacy. His influence continues to reverberate through the industry, inspiring musicians to explore new sonic territories and challenging the norms of what electronic music can be. Rusko's impact on the music industry will be felt for generations to come, ensuring his place as a true sonic legend.

# A Future of Sonic Innovation

## Exploring New Frontiers

In the search for sonic innovation, Rusko is constantly pushing the boundaries of electronic music. He is known for his fearless exploration of different genres and his ability to create groundbreaking sounds that captivate audiences around the world. In this section, we will delve into Rusko's journey of experimentation and his quest to redefine what is possible in the realm of electronic music.

## Breaking the Mold

Rusko has always been one to challenge conventions and break the mold. He constantly seeks out new frontiers and is unafraid to venture into uncharted territories. One of his most notable endeavors in exploring new sonic landscapes is his foray into the realm of ambient electronica.

Ambient electronica is a genre that emphasizes the creation of immersive and atmospheric soundscapes. It is characterized by its ethereal melodies and minimalistic approach. Rusko embraced this genre as a canvas for his sonic experimentation and created mesmerizing compositions that are evocative and thought-provoking.

To achieve the desired atmospheric effects, Rusko employed various techniques such as layering and manipulating sounds, incorporating field recordings, and using unconventional instruments. He seamlessly blended organic elements with electronic textures, resulting in a truly unique sonic experience.

## Blurring the Lines

Rusko is not content with simply exploring different genres; he is also passionate about blurring the lines between them. By fusing disparate musical styles, he creates hybrid compositions that defy categorization. This approach has led to the emergence of groundbreaking sub-genres that challenge traditional notions of music.

One such example is Rusko's exploration of the intersection between dubstep and jazz. At first glance, these two genres may seem incompatible, but Rusko saw potential in their fusion. He incorporated elements of jazz, such as improvisation and complex rhythms, into his dubstep productions, resulting in a truly innovative sound.

This amalgamation of genres not only expands the sonic palette of electronic music but also opens up new possibilities for collaboration and creativity. Rusko's willingness to experiment and think outside the box has inspired countless artists to embrace unconventional approaches and explore new avenues in their own music.

## The Power of Technology

In Rusko's quest to explore new frontiers, technology plays a crucial role. He embraces the latest advancements in music production tools and software to push the boundaries of what is sonically possible. Through the use of cutting-edge equipment and techniques, he is able to create sounds that were once unimaginable.

One example of Rusko's technological innovation is his use of granular synthesis. This technique involves breaking down sound into tiny grains and manipulating them to create new textures and timbres. By harnessing the power of granular synthesis, Rusko has been able to craft intricate and otherworldly soundscapes that transport listeners to new dimensions.

Furthermore, Rusko leverages the power of live performance technology to enhance his shows and create immersive experiences for his audience. He incorporates visual projections, interactive lighting, and synchronized effects to elevate his performances to a whole new level. Through the integration of technology, Rusko blurs the lines between auditory and visual art, leaving a lasting impact on his fans.

## Embracing the Unknown

To explore new frontiers, one must be willing to embrace the unknown. Rusko continually challenges himself to step outside of his comfort zone and venture into unexplored territories. He seeks inspiration from unlikely sources and is unafraid of failure.

Rusko's relentless pursuit of sonic innovation has led him to collaborate with artists from diverse backgrounds and genres. By collaborating with musicians outside of his usual sphere, he introduces new ideas and perspectives into his creative process, resulting in fresh and exciting musical ventures.

Moreover, Rusko actively seeks out unconventional performance spaces to create unique and immersive experiences for his audience. From abandoned warehouses to open-air locations, he breaks free from the confines of traditional venues, transforming ordinary spaces into extraordinary sonic landscapes.

## Looking Ahead

As Rusko continues to explore new frontiers, the future holds endless possibilities. His insatiable curiosity and drive to push the boundaries of electronic music guarantee that his sonic innovation will never cease.

With emerging technologies and the ever-evolving music landscape, there is an exciting future of sonic exploration on the horizon. Rusko's bold approach serves as an inspiration for aspiring artists to break free from conventions and embark on their own sonic journeys of discovery.

In conclusion, Rusko's exploration of new frontiers is a testament to his visionary spirit and relentless pursuit of sonic innovation. By delving into different genres, blurring the lines between them, harnessing the power of technology, embracing the unknown, and looking ahead, he remains at the forefront of electronic music, forever shaping its future.

## Vision for the Future

As Rusko looks towards the future of his music career, he envisions a sonic landscape filled with endless possibilities and boundless creativity. He sees himself embracing new technologies, innovative sounds, and unconventional genres to continue pushing the boundaries of electronic music. Rusko's vision for the future is not only about creating unique and captivating music, but also about inspiring and nurturing the next generation of artists.

One of the key aspects of Rusko's vision is the exploration of new frontiers in music production. He believes that technology can be a powerful tool for expanding the sonic palette and creating new and exciting musical experiences. From virtual reality concerts to interactive music installations, Rusko is eager to experiment with cutting-edge technologies to bring his music to life in innovative ways. He envisions concerts where the audience becomes fully immersed in the music, blurring the lines between the artist and the listener.

In order to achieve his vision, Rusko recognizes the importance of collaboration. He believes that true innovation happens when artists from different disciplines come together and bring their unique perspectives to the table. Rusko plans to collaborate with visual artists, filmmakers, and even scientists to create multidimensional sensory experiences that go beyond the traditional bounds of music. By combining the power of music with other art forms, he aims to create unforgettable and transformative experiences for his fans.

Furthermore, Rusko envisions his music becoming a catalyst for social change and collective introspection. He recognizes that music has the power to bring people together, and he wants to use his platform to address pressing social issues and inspire positive change. Whether it's through thought-provoking lyrics, collaborations with activist artists, or fundraising efforts for important causes, Rusko wants his music to become a vehicle for spreading awareness and making a difference in the world.

In order to achieve his vision for the future, Rusko understands the importance of continuous learning and growth as an artist. He plans to dedicate time to studying and experimenting with different musical traditions from around the world. By incorporating elements of diverse musical cultures into his own work, he hopes to create a truly global sonic tapestry that resonates with listeners from all walks of life.

A FUTURE OF SONIC INNOVATION                                           111

As Rusko embarks on this journey into the future, he understands that challenges and obstacles will inevitably arise. However, he remains committed to pushing through these difficulties, knowing that they are essential for personal and artistic growth. He encourages aspiring musicians to embrace failure as a learning opportunity and to take risks in order to discover their own unique artistic voices.

In conclusion, Rusko's vision for the future encompasses an exploration of new technologies, collaborations across different art forms, and a dedication to social change. By embracing these ideas, he aims to create music that not only entertains but also challenges and inspires. Through his relentless pursuit of sonic innovation, Rusko hopes to leave a lasting impact on the music industry and inspire future generations of artists to think outside the box and push the boundaries of what is possible. As he continues to evolve and experiment, the future of Rusko's music promises to be an exciting and unpredictable journey into uncharted sonic dimensions.

## Anticipation for Upcoming Projects

As Rusko embarks on the next phase of his musical journey, fans and critics alike eagerly anticipate his upcoming projects. Always pushing the boundaries of sonic exploration, he continues to captivate audiences with his innovative style and genre-defying compositions. In this section, we will delve into the anticipation surrounding Rusko's future releases, his plans for collaboration, and his vision for the future of electronic music.

### Embracing Evolution

Rusko has never been one to rest on his laurels. Throughout his career, he has constantly evolved and experimented with different sounds and genres. As he looks toward the future, he is set to take his sonic exploration to new heights, incorporating elements from diverse musical styles and infusing them with his signature electronic beats. This fusion of influences promises to create a fresh and exciting sound that pushes the boundaries of electronic music.

### Collaborations that Push Boundaries

One of the most anticipated aspects of Rusko's upcoming projects is his collaborations with a variety of artists from different genres. By teaming up with musicians who have their own unique styles and perspectives, Rusko aims to create synergistic collaborations that result in groundbreaking tracks. Whether it's collaborating with established artists or discovering new talent, Rusko's collaborations are sure to push the boundaries of electronic music and create truly memorable sonic experiences.

## Innovative Production Techniques

As an accomplished producer, Rusko has always been at the forefront of innovative production techniques. In his upcoming projects, he plans to continue pushing the envelope by exploring new ways to manipulate sound and create immersive sonic landscapes. From experimenting with unconventional sampling methods to utilizing cutting-edge technology, Rusko's dedication to sonic innovation promises to deliver unparalleled musical experiences.

## Connecting with the Audience

Throughout his career, Rusko has developed a strong connection with his audience, and he plans to further strengthen this bond in his upcoming projects. By incorporating interactive elements into his live performances and exploring new ways to engage with his fans, he aims to create an immersive and unforgettable experience for concertgoers. With the advancements in technology, Rusko envisions a future where concerts transcend the traditional boundaries of music, combining visual art, immersive installations, and interactive experiences to create multisensory events that leave a lasting impression.

## Shaping the Future of Electronic Music

Rusko's influence on electronic music cannot be overstated, and he continues to play a pivotal role in shaping the genre's future. With his upcoming projects, he strives to inspire and empower the next generation of electronic music artists. Through collaborations, mentorship programs, and sharing his insights and knowledge, Rusko aims to create a supportive and nurturing environment for aspiring musicians. By encouraging experimentation and pushing the boundaries of what is possible, he hopes to pave the way for a future where electronic music is constantly evolving and pushing the limits of sonic expression.

## An Unconventional Challenge

To further challenge his artistic boundaries and stimulate his creative process, Rusko has decided to launch a unique project alongside his upcoming releases. This project will involve collaborating with renowned visual artists to create a series of immersive music videos that intertwine with the music itself. By blurring the lines between music, film, and visual art, Rusko aims to create a truly groundbreaking and unforgettable multimedia experience.

## Pushing Societal Boundaries

In addition to his musical projects, Rusko is actively involved in tackling social issues and raising awareness through his platform. With his upcoming projects, he plans to use his influence and reach to shed light on pressing societal concerns. From advocating for environmental sustainability to promoting mental health awareness, Rusko aims to inspire positive change through his music and actions.

## Challenging the Status Quo

Rusko's upcoming projects will undoubtedly challenge the status quo of the music industry. By eschewing traditional distribution models and embracing innovative approaches, he aims to redefine success in the digital age. From exploring new platforms for releasing music to experimenting with alternative revenue streams, Rusko's vision for the future of the music industry is both exciting and disruptive.

In conclusion, as Rusko embarks on his latest musical endeavors, the anticipation for his upcoming projects is palpable. Through his commitment to sonic exploration, collaborations, innovative production techniques, and connecting with his audience, he is set to leave an indelible mark on electronic music. By embracing the unknown, pushing boundaries, and challenging societal norms, Rusko is poised to shape the future of not only his own sound but the entire genre. With his upcoming releases, the world eagerly awaits to embark on this sonic journey with him, ready to be inspired and captivated by his groundbreaking music.

## Rusko's Enduring Influence

Rusko's impact on the music industry has been nothing short of revolutionary. His unique sound and innovative approach to electronic music have left an indelible mark on the genre and continue to inspire a new generation of artists. In this section, we will explore the enduring influence of Rusko and delve into his contributions to the sonic landscape.

One of the key aspects of Rusko's enduring influence is his ability to bridge the gap between different genres and musical styles. Throughout his career, he has seamlessly incorporated elements of dubstep, reggae, hip-hop, and drum and bass into his music. This fusion of genres has not only expanded the sonic possibilities of electronic music but has also opened doors for artists to experiment and collaborate across different musical worlds.

To fully understand Rusko's enduring influence, it is important to explore his collaborative efforts with other artists. Rusko's willingness to work with musicians from diverse backgrounds has not only elevated his own sound but has also allowed for the creation of innovative and groundbreaking music. His collaborations with artists such as Cypress Hill, SuChin Pak, and Selah Sue have resulted in tracks that push the boundaries of what is possible within the electronic music landscape.

In addition to his collaborations, Rusko's production skills and unique approach to live performances have had a lasting impact on the music industry. His ability to create infectious, bass-driven hooks combined with expertly crafted sound design has set a new standard for electronic music production. Artists across the globe have been influenced by his signature sound and strive to emulate his ability to create mesmerizing and energetic tracks.

Rusko's live performances are a spectacle in and of themselves. Known for his high-energy sets and seamless mixing, he has captivated audiences around the world. His ability to create an immersive and unforgettable experience through his live performances has influenced other artists to step up their game and deliver electrifying shows. From his dynamic stage presence to his use of live improvisation, Rusko has set a new standard for what it means to be a live electronic music artist.

Beyond his contributions to the sonic landscape, Rusko's enduring influence can also be seen in his dedicated fanbase. His music has resonated with listeners on an emotional level, creating a deep connection that transcends boundaries. The passion and loyalty of his fans are a testament to the profound impact his music has had on their lives. Artists who inspire such devotion are rare, and Rusko's ability to forge a deep connection with his audience speaks volumes about his lasting influence.

In conclusion, Rusko's enduring influence is multifaceted and far-reaching. Through his unique sound, collaborations with other artists, expert production skills, and captivating live performances, he has left an indelible mark on the music industry. His ability to push the boundaries of electronic music and create a connection with his fans sets him apart as a true sonic legend. As electronic music continues to evolve, Rusko's influence will undoubtedly continue to resonate, shaping the future of the genre and inspiring generations of artists to come.

# Conclusion

## Rusko: A Sonic Phenomenon Explored

### Impact on Electronic Music

Rusko's impact on electronic music cannot be understated. His unique sound and innovative approach have left an indelible mark on the genre, inspiring countless artists and shaping the landscape of electronic music as we know it today.

1. Redefining Dubstep: Rusko played a pivotal role in redefining dubstep, pushing its boundaries and infusing it with his distinctive style. By incorporating elements of reggae, hip-hop, and drum and bass, he brought a fresh perspective to the genre, expanding its sonic possibilities and attracting a wider audience. His signature high-energy beats and infectious basslines became synonymous with dubstep, creating a new sound that reverberated through clubs, festivals, and headphones.

2. Mainstream Breakthrough: Rusko's infectious tunes and energetic performances catapulted him into the mainstream spotlight. He played a crucial role in introducing dubstep to a wider audience, with hits like "Cockney Thug" and "Woo Boost" gaining massive popularity. His music reached the top of the charts, exposing millions of listeners to the raw power and infectious energy of electronic music.

3. Bridging the Gap: One of Rusko's greatest contributions was his ability to bridge the gap between underground electronic music and the mainstream. He introduced a new generation to the electrifying sounds of dubstep, making it accessible to a wider audience without compromising its authenticity. By collaborating with mainstream artists and integrating his signature sound into popular culture, he paved the way for electronic music to be recognized as a true art form.

4. Live Performances: Rusko's live performances were legendary, captivating

audiences with his infectious energy and unparalleled stage presence. His ability to seamlessly blend genres and deliver mind-blowing drops created an immersive experience that left a lasting impact on concertgoers. Rusko's stage presence and dynamic performances redefined what it meant to experience electronic music live, setting new standards for the industry.

5. Innovation and Evolution: Beyond his initial breakthrough, Rusko continued to innovate and evolve, constantly pushing the boundaries of electronic music. His experimentation with different genres and willingness to explore new sonic territories challenged the status quo, inspiring a new wave of artists to think outside the box. Rusko's influence can be heard in the work of artists spanning various sub-genres, from future bass to trap, demonstrating the lasting impact of his sonic exploration.

6. Inspiring Future Artists: Rusko's impact on electronic music extends far beyond his own success. His groundbreaking sound and trailblazing career have inspired a new generation of electronic music producers and DJs. The innovation and creativity he brought to the industry serve as a constant reminder that pushing boundaries and taking risks can lead to unparalleled success. From basement studios to festival stages, Rusko's influence can be felt throughout the electronic music community.

In conclusion, Rusko's impact on electronic music is immeasurable. Through his unique sound, mainstream breakthrough, and innovative approach, he has redefined dubstep and paved the way for electronic music to take center stage. His influence continues to shape the industry, inspiring future artists to push the boundaries and explore new sonic dimensions. Rusko's legacy as a sonic legend is not just confined to his own success but is deeply ingrained in the fabric of electronic music itself.

## Inspiring the Next Generation

As Rusko's career has unfolded, one thing has become abundantly clear: his music has had a profound impact on the next generation of musicians and artists. His innovative style, fearlessness in exploring new sonic dimensions, and unwavering dedication to his craft have served as an inspiration for countless aspiring musicians. In this section, we will delve into the ways in which Rusko has inspired the next generation and how his unique approach continues to shape the music industry.

## Pushing Boundaries

Rusko's ability to push the boundaries of electronic music has captivated the minds of young musicians looking to break free from the constraints of tradition. By fearlessly blending various genres and styles, he has paved the way for a new era of sonic exploration and expanded the possibilities of what electronic music can be.

Young artists who once felt limited by predefined genres and notions of what music should sound like are now emboldened to experiment and challenge the status quo. Rusko's willingness to take risks and embrace unconventional sounds has given them permission to explore uncharted territory, fostering a new wave of creativity and innovation.

## Embracing Collaboration

Collaboration has become a hallmark of Rusko's career, and this approach has had a profound impact on the next generation of musicians. By working with artists from a variety of genres and backgrounds, Rusko has shown aspiring musicians the power of diversity and the endless possibilities that arise from collaboration.

His collaborations with hip-hop artists, rock bands, and even classical musicians have demonstrated that music knows no boundaries. As young musicians witness the beauty that emerges when different styles and perspectives meld together, they are encouraged to seek out their own collaborative partnerships and explore new sonic avenues.

## The DIY Mentality

Rusko's rise to fame is a testament to the do-it-yourself (DIY) mentality that resonates deeply with the next generation of musicians. From his early beginnings, he embraced the power of self-expression through music and took full control of his artistic journey.

By utilizing the internet and social media platforms to connect directly with fans, Rusko has dismantled traditional gatekeeping mechanisms and demonstrated that success can be achieved through grassroots efforts. This has inspired countless musicians to take charge of their own careers, embracing independent distribution models and using online platforms to build their own fanbase.

## Staying True to Yourself

Perhaps one of the most inspiring aspects of Rusko's journey is his unwavering commitment to staying true to himself. In a music industry that often pressures artists to conform to trends and commercial demands, Rusko has stayed authentic to his unique sound and artistic vision.

By not compromising his creative integrity, Rusko has shown young musicians the importance of remaining true to their own artistic pursuits. In a world that celebrates individuality and authenticity, his steadfast commitment to his craft serves as a beacon of hope for the next generation, reminding them that staying true to themselves can ultimately lead to long-lasting success and fulfillment.

## Breaking Down Barriers

Rusko's impact extends beyond the realm of music. As a prominent black artist in the electronic music scene, he has broken down barriers and opened doors for aspiring musicians from underrepresented communities.

His success serves as a powerful example of what can be achieved when barriers are dismantled and opportunities are made available to all. By inspiring a more diverse generation of musicians, Rusko has played a crucial role in reshaping the landscape of electronic music and ensuring its future remains vibrant and inclusive.

In conclusion, Rusko's influence on the next generation of musicians cannot be overstated. His innovative approach, fearlessness in pushing boundaries, emphasis on collaboration, DIY mentality, commitment to authenticity, and efforts to break down barriers have inspired and empowered aspiring musicians around the world. As electronic music continues to evolve, Rusko's legacy will undoubtedly live on, forever inspiring the next generation to explore new sonic dimensions and leave their own mark on the music industry.

## A Final Note on Rusko's Legacy

Rusko, the enigmatic sonic rebel who reshaped the landscape of electronic music, leaves behind a lasting legacy that continues to inspire and captivate audiences around the world. As we reflect on his remarkable career and the impact he has made, it becomes clear that his influence reaches far beyond his genre-defying sound. Rusko's legacy is one of artistic innovation, perseverance, and a relentless pursuit of sonic exploration.

At the heart of Rusko's legacy lies his unwavering commitment to pushing the boundaries of electronic music. Throughout his career, he fearlessly delved into different genres and styles, constantly challenging himself and his listeners. His ability to seamlessly blend dubstep, drum and bass, reggae, and other genres created a sonic landscape that was uniquely his own. Rusko showed the world that genres could be transcended and that music could be a limitless form of expression.

One of the most defining aspects of Rusko's legacy is his commitment to live performances. He understood the power of a captivating live show and went above and beyond to deliver unforgettable experiences to his fans. With his infectious energy and unparalleled stage presence, Rusko transformed each performance into a sonic journey that transcended the boundaries of traditional electronic music shows. His ability to connect with the crowd and create a sense of unity within the audience set him apart as a true sonic pioneer.

Rusko's enduring influence can be seen in the countless artists he has inspired and collaborated with. His willingness to break away from the norm and experiment with new sounds opened the doors for a new generation of musicians. The impact he has had on the music industry cannot be overstated. His music continues to be sampled, remixed, and celebrated by artists from across the globe, showcasing the timeless appeal of his creations.

But Rusko's legacy extends far beyond the world of music. His personal journey, marked by struggles with substance abuse and subsequent recovery, serves as a testament to his resilience and determination. Rusko's willingness to confront his demons head-on and seek help for his addiction has been an inspiration to many. Through his journey, he has shown that even in the face of adversity, it is possible to find healing and reclaim one's passion.

In addition to his musical achievements, Rusko's philanthropic endeavors have left a lasting impact on communities in need. Whether it be through charity concerts, donations, or advocacy, he used his platform to make a difference in the lives of others. Rusko's commitment to giving back serves as a reminder that artists have the power to create positive change and touch the lives of those who need it most.

As we look to the future, Rusko's legacy reminds us of the importance of embracing sonic innovation and pushing artistic boundaries. His relentless pursuit of new sounds and genres serves as a beacon of inspiration for aspiring musicians. His ability to challenge the status quo and reinvent himself time and time again showcases the importance of embracing change and staying true to one's artistic vision.

In conclusion, Rusko's legacy is one that will continue to reverberate through the halls of electronic music history. His artistic innovation, resilience, and commitment to sonic exploration have left an indelible mark on the genre and inspired countless artists. As we celebrate his achievements, let us remember to embrace the spirit of Rusko's legacy and continue to push the boundaries of music, just as he did. Let his enduring influence serve as a reminder that there are no limits to what can be achieved when we dare to think outside the box and embrace the power of sonic innovation. The world of music is forever changed by the irreplaceable contributions of Rusko, the sonic rebel who dared to challenge the status quo and redefine the possibilities of sound.

# Index

-doubt, 15, 71
2.3.1.1, 25

ability, 6, 7, 16, 17, 19–21, 23, 24,
    27, 30, 32, 37–39, 43, 44,
    46, 47, 49, 52–54, 57, 58,
    64, 66, 70, 75, 76, 78, 83,
    86–89, 91, 92, 95, 97–99,
    102, 105, 107, 113–117,
    119, 120
absence, 30
abuse, 16, 61–65, 67, 68, 70, 72, 80,
    92, 93, 119
acceptance, 42, 71
access, 31, 62
accessibility, 88
acclaim, 32, 47, 83
acronym, 2
act, 7, 27, 36, 57
action, 58
adaptability, 73
addiction, 61–65, 67–69, 80, 119
addition, 10, 17, 28, 38, 47, 56, 59,
    69, 80, 85, 101, 103, 105,
    113, 114, 119
Adele, 75
admiration, 31, 48, 104
adolescence, 10

adrenaline, 59
advent, 99
adventure, 10, 17, 18
adversity, 16, 49, 66, 69, 73, 74, 82,
    94, 96, 119
advice, 72
advocacy, 119
advocate, 62, 69
aesthetic, 58, 59, 100
affair, 10, 11, 13
afternoon, 53
age, 1, 3, 9, 11, 13, 54, 91, 113
aid, 30, 80
air, 1, 9, 55, 109
album, 15, 87
alchemy, 2
alcohol, 64
allure, 3, 64
amalgamation, 18, 108
Amber Coffman, 47
ambition, 53
America, 42
amplitude, 36
analog, 85
analysis, 59
anchor, 62
answer, 18, 36
anthem, 42, 105

Anthony Kiedis, 63
anticipation, 31, 54, 111, 113
Aphex Twin, 4, 10
appeal, 23, 37, 119
appearance, 42
appreciation, 5, 9, 13, 17, 44, 78, 99
approach, 2, 7, 18, 19, 22–25, 28, 30, 31, 38, 40, 45, 48, 49, 52, 63, 66, 71, 73, 74, 77, 78, 81–85, 87–89, 92, 96–102, 106–109, 113–118
area, 22, 29, 46, 98
array, 17, 55, 82
arrival, 54, 55
art, 20, 33, 57, 66, 69–71, 101, 102, 105, 109–113, 115
artist, 2, 3, 5–7, 9, 10, 12, 17, 18, 21, 23, 26, 31, 32, 39, 43, 46–48, 52, 55, 63, 69–72, 74, 75, 77, 79, 81–84, 87, 93–95, 99–101, 104, 105, 110, 114, 118
artistry, 2, 16, 62, 68
ascent, 7, 54
aspect, 38, 51, 57, 68, 81, 85, 102
assault, 27, 55
atmosphere, 29, 53, 54
attendance, 30
attention, 6, 14, 18, 24, 29, 31, 38, 48, 51, 53
attitude, 49, 82–84
audacity, 45, 48
audience, 6, 7, 15, 19, 23, 25, 27, 28, 30, 31, 36, 42, 46–48, 50–53, 55, 57, 58, 65, 66, 68, 69, 71, 75–77, 83, 85, 87, 93, 97, 100, 103, 105, 106, 109, 110, 112–115, 119
Australia, 43
Autechre, 4
authenticity, 25, 31, 68, 71, 78, 81, 82, 93, 95, 97, 107, 115, 118
avenue, 85
awareness, 62, 63, 67–69, 110, 113
awe, 26, 52, 55, 104, 105

backbone, 10
backdrop, 57
background, 1, 9–11, 14, 19, 71, 76, 91
backlash, 48–51
backyard, 4
balance, 28, 49, 55, 65, 66, 73, 93, 94
balancing, 7, 95
ball, 30
band, 104
banger, 46
basement, 11, 116
basketball, 23
bass, 4, 10, 16–18, 21, 24, 27, 31, 32, 36–38, 44, 48, 49, 53, 55, 58, 73, 83, 84, 87, 88, 97, 99, 100, 102, 104, 106, 113–116, 119
bassline, 36
battle, 61–63, 67, 80
beacon, 96, 118, 120
beast, 45
beat, 10, 12, 20, 31, 50, 55, 57
beauty, 20, 85, 96, 117
bedroom, 11, 27
beginning, 11, 42, 70, 74
being, 15, 23, 52, 61, 63, 64, 67–70, 74, 80, 82, 91, 94, 95
belief, 63, 96, 105

belonging, 30
bending, 2, 4, 7, 23, 27, 36, 47, 58, 83, 88, 104
Benga, 22, 36, 40
Beyoncé, 58
biography, 48
birth, 2, 12, 25, 26, 83
birthplace, 1, 3, 9–11, 36
blend, 6, 7, 10, 12, 14, 16, 18, 27, 31, 37, 38, 41, 44, 46–48, 52, 54, 70, 75, 76, 83, 84, 91, 97, 102, 105, 116, 119
blending, 2, 20, 24, 26, 29, 32, 37, 41, 47, 50, 51, 54, 58, 82, 84, 85, 97, 101, 106, 117
blueprint, 88
Bob Marley, 22
body, 67, 74
bolt, 11
bond, 30, 53, 81, 103, 112
bone, 36
book, 12
boom, 87
bound, 45
boundary, 4, 38, 54, 59, 75, 83, 85, 86
box, 19, 23, 51, 57, 76, 102, 105, 106, 108, 111, 116, 120
breakbeat, 31
breaking, 24, 28, 57, 65, 76, 77, 84, 104, 109
breakout, 46
breakthrough, 7, 27, 41–43, 116
Brian Eno, 10
bridge, 39, 71, 75, 97, 113, 115
brilliance, 48
brim, 55
brostep, 100
building, 6, 30, 42, 73, 103

burnout, 66
buzzing, 85

cacophony, 12, 79
cafe, 20
call, 104
calling, 11, 91
camaraderie, 30
Canada, 43
canvas, 44, 108
capacity, 16
capsule, 5
car, 79, 85
care, 63, 67, 80, 94–96
career, 7, 10, 12, 14–17, 21, 25, 26, 31, 38, 39, 44, 52, 61, 64, 66, 68, 69, 72, 74, 76, 80, 82–84, 86, 88, 91–94, 96, 100, 104, 106, 110–113, 116, 117, 119
Caspa, 40, 75, 100
cast, 2
catalog, 46
catalyst, 43, 50, 62, 72, 102, 110
categorization, 22, 26, 32, 38, 57, 75, 83–85, 108
category, 56
cause, 62
challenge, 2, 4, 5, 17–19, 25, 45, 50, 64, 65, 73–75, 77, 97, 101, 103, 106, 108, 112, 113, 117, 120
chance, 52, 53
change, 2, 26, 57, 62, 66, 67, 71, 85, 97, 110, 111, 113, 119, 120
changer, 36, 74
channel, 24, 95
chaos, 62

chapter, 1, 2, 6, 12, 26, 37, 39, 48, 61, 64, 67–69, 74, 79–82, 105
characteristic, 11
charge, 117
charisma, 55
charity, 119
chart, 7, 40, 46–48, 50, 58, 75, 97
chatter, 20
child, 3, 12, 13, 91
childhood, 10
Chinwe Gonzalez, 39
choice, 23, 82, 96
chord, 11, 46
chorus, 19
Chris Woodstra, 29
circuit, 7, 52
city, 9, 10, 12, 13, 19, 20, 32, 33, 79
clarity, 62, 65, 70, 72, 81
classic, 42, 104
clinking, 85
close, 1, 62, 105
club, 31, 36, 42, 46, 54, 55
Coachella, 42
Coffman, 47
collaboration, 4, 6, 15, 19, 21–23, 39–41, 44, 46, 47, 51, 71, 72, 74–76, 78, 83, 84, 88, 96, 97, 103–105, 108, 110, 111, 117, 118
collaborator, 102
collection, 1, 3, 10–12, 99
collide, 38, 48
collision, 5
combination, 10, 50
comeback, 72, 73
comfort, 18, 40, 78, 92, 96, 109
commercial, 28, 47, 49, 65, 107, 118
commercialization, 48

commitment, 16, 18, 26, 29, 31, 39, 45, 52, 57, 68, 69, 74, 78, 80, 85, 87, 92, 93, 102, 103, 106, 107, 113, 117–120
communication, 81
community, 1, 13, 21, 22, 24, 28, 30, 52, 63, 81, 89, 94, 102, 103, 107, 116
companion, 11, 58
component, 84
composer, 83
composition, 79, 100
concept, 85
concern, 62
concert, 30
conclusion, 7, 26, 41, 47, 52, 54, 55, 57, 74, 82, 85, 87, 92, 98, 103, 107, 109, 111, 113, 114, 116, 118, 120
confidant, 11
confidence, 14, 65
conflict, 28
confluence, 5, 39
conformity, 29, 45, 95
connection, 12, 25, 26, 47, 55, 62, 73, 81, 85, 87, 94, 103, 112, 114
conquest, 42
consciousness, 4, 28
constellation, 3
constraint, 85
consumption, 49
contemporary, 51, 58, 100
content, 17, 24, 27, 30, 31, 45, 77, 108
contribution, 89, 100
control, 28, 65, 68, 70
controversy, 51

*Index* 125

convenience, 39
convention, 2, 56
conversation, 63
cookie, 45
core, 18, 37, 94, 99
corner, 10, 98
cornerstone, 93, 100
counseling, 62, 68, 80
country, 27, 39, 42
courage, 66, 67, 81
course, 62
crackling, 11
craft, 6, 10, 12, 13, 15, 16, 18, 26–29, 39, 47, 52, 54, 67–69, 71, 77, 80, 88, 95, 109, 116, 118
creation, 23, 38, 40, 57, 84, 85, 108, 114
creative, 2, 4, 5, 7, 9, 14, 15, 20, 23, 24, 28, 33, 39–41, 45, 48, 49, 64–66, 70–73, 76, 81, 91, 100, 106, 109, 112, 118
creativity, 1, 6, 10, 12, 18–21, 24, 36, 38, 43–46, 49, 50, 54, 55, 64–68, 70–72, 74, 76, 84, 94, 96, 97, 101–103, 108, 110, 116, 117
crispness, 38
criticism, 15, 29, 49, 50, 57
cross, 40, 78, 88, 98
crosswalk, 79
crowd, 25, 27, 29, 43, 50, 52–55, 119
crystal, 30
culmination, 52
cultivation, 82
culture, 4, 13, 39, 51, 52, 58, 59, 63, 64, 98, 99, 115

curiosity, 1, 10, 11, 13, 17, 31, 91, 100, 109
custom, 36, 56
cutoff, 36
cutter, 45
cutting, 53, 56, 72, 77, 101, 108, 110, 112
cybergoth, 59
cycle, 62
Cypress Hill, 75, 114

dance, 4, 20, 53, 54
dancefloor, 2, 30
dancing, 48, 50, 55
data, 30
day, 11, 13, 28, 52, 56, 65
deal, 7, 65, 87
debate, 48
debut, 87
decision, 65, 67, 70, 92
dedication, 7, 16, 46, 52, 54, 69, 74, 92–94, 96, 100, 103, 107, 111, 112, 116
Deep, 75
demand, 50, 64
demeanor, 49
depth, 32, 39, 71, 74
desert, 55
design, 24, 38, 48, 84, 99, 100, 102, 114
desire, 21, 31, 41, 50, 85, 94, 100
destigmatization, 63
destiny, 2
detail, 18, 24, 38
determination, 6, 7, 14, 15, 26, 33, 36, 43, 49, 62–66, 72, 74, 92, 93, 107, 119
deterrent, 50
detoxification, 65, 70

development, 4, 9, 44, 61, 76, 88, 93, 94, 100
deviation, 48
devotion, 31, 114
difference, 110, 119
Digital Mystikz, 22
dimension, 38, 48, 53, 68
Diplo, 58
direction, 63, 81
disappointment, 61
discipline, 71
discography, 29, 46, 89
discovery, 2, 3, 16, 26, 69, 71, 109
discussion, 5
disdain, 48
dissonance, 49
distribution, 106, 113, 117
dive, 37, 38, 46, 52
diversity, 10, 24, 39, 77, 83, 84, 100, 102, 103, 117
DJ, 15
domain, 84
domination, 30, 46, 47
door, 19, 52
dose, 46
doubt, 15, 71
down, 24, 46, 49, 67, 75–77, 80, 102, 104, 105, 109, 118
dreamer, 12
dribbling, 23
drill, 58
drive, 1, 10, 21, 25, 28, 109
drum, 4, 16–18, 21, 24, 27, 31, 32, 37, 38, 44, 53, 83, 84, 87, 97, 99, 100, 102, 106, 113, 115, 119
drummer, 79
dub, 10, 17, 18, 27, 99, 102

dubstep, 4, 5, 7, 10, 11, 14–18, 21–23, 26, 27, 32, 35–45, 47–49, 51, 53, 54, 58, 59, 73–77, 82–84, 87–89, 91, 97–101, 104, 106, 108, 113, 115, 116, 119
duo, 40
dynamic, 7, 19, 21, 32, 40, 42, 47, 51, 52, 56, 77, 85, 98, 100, 106, 114, 116

eagerness, 21
ear, 24, 32
Eastern Europe, 25
ecosystem, 36
edge, 53, 56, 72, 77, 101, 108, 110, 112
edition, 31
education, 10, 11
effect, 107
effort, 62, 73
electronic, 2–7, 10–13, 19, 21, 22, 24, 26–29, 32, 36, 37, 39–44, 46, 47, 49–52, 54, 56–59, 70, 72–78, 82, 84–89, 91, 92, 96–99, 101–120
electronica, 77, 108
element, 7, 23, 55, 98
Ellie Goulding, 41
embrace, 10, 14, 33, 43, 45, 49, 56, 66, 76–78, 84, 86, 89, 93, 95, 100–102, 105–109, 111, 117, 120
Emeli Sandé, 58, 75
emergence, 44, 58, 59, 65, 100, 108
emotion, 88
empathy, 63, 81
emphasis, 99, 118

# Index

encounter, 10, 15
encouragement, 67, 72
end, 20
endeavor, 31
energy, 2, 4, 7, 9, 17, 20, 26, 29, 32, 37, 43, 44, 46, 47, 49–55, 58, 73, 83, 88, 97–100, 104, 114–116, 119
engine, 85
England, 4, 13, 35
enigma, 1, 3, 11, 12, 37
entertainment, 51
enthusiasm, 22, 43, 55, 68
envelope, 48, 105, 112
environment, 23, 44, 66, 99, 112
equilibrium, 95
equipment, 1, 108
era, 38, 117
escape, 36, 61
essence, 2, 20, 25, 36, 66, 84
ethic, 64
ethos, 59
euphoria, 47
event, 29
everyday, 12, 23, 24, 78, 85, 103
evolution, 12, 17, 25, 26, 29, 37, 39, 40, 43, 46, 48, 50–52, 73, 77, 82, 84, 85, 89, 99–101, 103
example, 19, 75, 77, 78, 83, 84, 101–103, 108, 109, 118
excellence, 107
exception, 23, 48, 62, 64, 67, 74
exchange, 31, 40, 100
excitement, 31, 50, 51, 53, 98
exclusivity, 31
exercise, 94
expectation, 64
expense, 93

experience, 7, 9, 11, 19, 22, 24, 25, 27, 28, 32, 38, 43, 47, 50–57, 59, 62, 64, 72, 73, 75, 77, 84, 85, 93, 102, 104, 106, 108, 112–114, 116
experiment, 10, 17–19, 21, 23, 24, 26, 27, 29, 31, 38, 40, 41, 49, 70, 72, 79, 83–85, 87–89, 97, 102, 103, 106–108, 110, 111, 114, 117, 119
experimentation, 11, 12, 17–21, 24, 25, 31, 33, 44, 46, 50, 51, 66, 73–76, 78, 82–84, 86, 88, 100, 102, 103, 107, 108, 112, 116
expert, 32, 114
expertise, 76, 106
exploration, 2–5, 7, 10–12, 17–21, 23, 25, 26, 28, 37, 39, 43, 45, 51, 52, 70, 72, 75–77, 81–87, 89, 92, 97, 99–101, 105, 107–111, 113, 116, 117, 119, 120
explore, 5, 9, 10, 12, 17–19, 21–26, 29, 31, 37, 39–41, 43–46, 48–50, 52, 57, 58, 72, 77, 83, 84, 87–89, 92–94, 96, 98–101, 103–109, 113, 114, 116–118
explosion, 74
exposure, 6, 9, 10, 21, 45, 102
expression, 6, 9, 23, 25, 33, 49, 62, 66, 84, 95, 112, 119
extravaganza, 53

fabric, 2, 10, 116
face, 69, 74, 95, 96, 119

factor, 47
fad, 48
failure, 14, 109, 111
fame, 1, 6, 7, 12, 26, 42, 43, 61, 63–67, 80, 87, 91
familiarity, 65
family, 1, 9–11, 13, 31, 62, 91
fan, 30, 51, 81
fanbase, 6, 27, 28, 30–32, 37, 42, 45, 47–49, 53, 73, 79, 81, 82, 95, 106, 114, 117
fascination, 101
fashion, 51, 58, 59
father, 11, 12
favor, 58
favorite, 29, 47, 51
façade, 93
fearlessness, 4, 88, 116, 118
feast, 29, 30, 105
feel, 29–31
feeling, 66
fervor, 30
festival, 7, 42, 52–55, 116
fi, 59
field, 79, 108
figure, 1, 6, 24, 47, 99, 100
film, 37, 58, 113
filter, 36
finish, 19
fire, 11, 14, 18, 48
fit, 98
flame, 66
flavor, 74, 78
Flosstradamus, 58
flow, 1, 50
fly, 56, 85
folklore, 25
following, 20, 23, 30
foot, 52

footage, 73
footing, 27
foray, 108
force, 1, 5, 6, 11, 12, 16, 32, 42, 99
forefront, 11, 21, 26, 37, 39, 56, 110, 112
forest, 101
form, 5, 10, 21, 33, 62, 68, 115, 119
format, 19
formula, 37
forum, 30
foundation, 1, 3, 5, 9, 10, 12, 23, 32, 44, 64, 88, 91, 99
freedom, 26, 70
frenzy, 55
frequency, 36
frontman, 63, 104
frustration, 61
fuel, 14, 15, 23, 71, 97
fulfillment, 67, 95, 118
fundraising, 110
funk, 3, 9, 17
fusion, 21, 23, 24, 27, 29, 31, 37, 38, 44, 45, 51, 58, 70, 74, 75, 77, 83, 85, 87, 88, 98, 99, 104, 106, 108, 111, 113
future, 1, 7, 12, 21, 32, 38, 39, 45, 54, 73, 74, 87–89, 92, 101, 103, 106, 107, 109–114, 116, 118, 120

game, 36, 56, 74, 114
gameplay, 59
gaming, 59
gap, 39, 41, 57, 58, 75, 97, 113, 115
garage, 4, 27, 35, 40
gatekeeping, 117
generation, 3, 7, 37, 39, 41, 43, 45, 49, 54, 57, 76, 84, 85, 89,

*Index*

97, 98, 105–107, 110, 112, 113, 115–119
genius, 25, 96
genre, 7, 10, 17, 18, 21–24, 26, 29, 31, 36–44, 46–49, 51, 54, 58, 59, 73, 75–77, 82–85, 87, 88, 91, 97–101, 103, 105, 106, 108, 111–115, 119, 120
glamour, 63
glance, 108
glass, 24
glimpse, 2
glitter, 64
glitz, 63
globe, 7, 43, 105, 114, 119
goal, 84
gold, 64
grail, 23
grandeur, 10, 104
gravity, 53
great, 17, 22, 87, 93, 98, 99
greatness, 45, 64
greet, 30
grime, 27
grip, 61, 64, 65
groove, 47
ground, 4, 9, 13, 40
groundbreaking, 4, 6, 12, 15, 19, 21–23, 28, 37, 41, 43, 58, 65, 74–76, 87–89, 99, 104, 105, 107, 108, 111, 113, 114, 116
groundwork, 12, 88
group, 75
growth, 14–16, 48, 50, 63, 68, 69, 71, 72, 77, 80, 81, 87, 91–96, 110, 111
Gucci Mane, 75

Gucci Mane's, 75
guidance, 93
guide, 5, 23, 72, 76
guitar, 11, 100
guitarist, 79

hallmark, 10, 117
hand, 25, 48, 63
Hans Zimmer's, 37
happiness, 95
hardware, 12, 18, 100
harmony, 55
haven, 1
head, 48, 65, 67, 68, 93, 119
headliner, 52–54
headlining, 3, 7, 50, 52–54
healing, 70, 119
health, 63–65, 67, 80, 95, 113
heart, 5, 20, 21, 36, 119
heartbeat, 9
helm, 38
help, 16, 24, 62, 64, 67, 70, 80, 91–93, 106, 119
heritage, 9, 10, 13, 25
hiatus, 73
high, 4, 17, 31, 47, 53, 58, 98, 100, 105, 114, 115
hip, 2, 5, 9, 13, 17, 18, 21, 23, 28, 36, 37, 44, 47, 53, 58, 75, 77, 82, 83, 85, 88, 91, 97, 99, 100, 105, 106, 113, 115, 117
history, 4, 10, 49, 99, 107, 120
hit, 21, 31, 40, 41, 46–48, 50, 70, 75
homage, 2, 25
home, 9, 55
hometown, 99
hop, 2, 5, 9, 13, 17, 18, 21, 23, 28, 36, 37, 44, 47, 53, 58, 75,

77, 82, 83, 85, 88, 91, 97, 99, 100, 105, 106, 113, 115, 117
hope, 62, 68, 73, 118
horizon, 33, 109
hotbed, 10
hour, 69
house, 40, 88
household, 9, 23, 39
hub, 30
humility, 68
hunger, 5, 10–12, 18
hurdle, 80
hybridity, 77
hype, 50

icon, 98
identity, 2, 4, 5, 18, 21, 25, 26, 31, 43–46, 66, 91, 99, 100
idol, 30
imagination, 20, 91
impact, 5, 7, 19, 26, 29, 35–39, 41, 43, 46, 47, 51, 52, 54, 55, 58, 59, 61, 63, 64, 66, 71, 74, 80, 82, 84, 87–89, 91, 92, 94, 97, 98, 101, 103, 106, 107, 109, 111, 113–119
importance, 23, 25, 31, 36, 48, 50, 53, 63, 66, 69, 70, 72, 73, 77, 80, 93, 95, 96, 102, 106, 107, 110, 118, 120
impression, 7, 29, 53, 54, 112
imprint, 97
improvement, 93
improvisation, 85, 98, 108, 114
inability, 61
inclusion, 58, 102
incorporation, 51, 58, 71, 85

independence, 49
individual, 3, 93, 100
individuality, 23, 45, 95, 118
industry, 3, 6–8, 14, 15, 26, 28, 29, 31, 42, 43, 45, 46, 53, 54, 59, 61, 63–65, 67, 69, 70, 74, 76, 78–82, 84, 87, 89, 91–98, 101–103, 106, 107, 111, 113, 114, 116–119
infiltration, 58
influence, 7, 9, 37, 39, 45, 56–59, 71, 76, 84, 87–89, 92, 97, 98, 101–103, 106, 107, 112–114, 116, 118–120
ingredient, 6
injection, 85
innovation, 3, 5, 12, 14, 15, 18, 22–24, 26, 38, 39, 43, 45, 52, 56, 57, 65, 66, 71, 74, 75, 78, 84, 85, 87, 92, 97, 101, 107, 109–112, 116, 117, 119, 120
innovator, 24, 44, 89, 101
insight, 12, 63
inspiration, 3–5, 8–14, 16–23, 25, 26, 43–46, 50, 59, 63, 65, 66, 71, 73, 77, 78, 82, 83, 85, 87–89, 92, 96, 97, 101, 102, 107, 109, 116, 119, 120
instance, 23, 78
instant, 28, 32, 41, 42, 47
instrument, 11, 24, 56
instrumentation, 51, 52, 56, 70, 75
integration, 51, 109
integrity, 7, 28, 48, 107, 118
intensity, 4, 59, 98
interaction, 30, 53

*Index*

interest, 22
internet, 117
intersection, 105, 108
intervention, 62
interview, 63
intimacy, 55, 73
introspection, 62, 66, 82, 93, 110
invincibility, 93
island, 1
issue, 64, 69
it, 1, 2, 4, 5, 9, 12, 14, 16, 18–20, 25, 28–30, 32, 33, 36, 37, 39, 44–46, 49, 52–59, 61–63, 66, 67, 69, 71, 72, 75, 76, 78, 80, 82, 84, 87, 91, 93, 96–98, 100, 101, 110, 111, 114–116, 119

Jahova, 24
jam, 9, 22
Japan, 43
jazz, 9, 11, 13, 44, 85, 108
Jimi Hendrix, 11
journey, 1–3, 5, 6, 9–12, 14–19, 21–23, 25–27, 30, 31, 33, 36, 37, 39, 41, 43, 45, 46, 49–52, 54–57, 61–64, 66–73, 76, 79–82, 84, 85, 91–97, 99–101, 103, 105, 107, 111, 113, 117, 119
joy, 65, 72
jumping, 55
jungle, 4, 14, 38, 48
juxtaposition, 58

kaleidoscope, 18
Kanye, 37
Katy Perry, 58

key, 6, 18, 24, 33, 38, 40, 42, 44, 47, 50, 81, 88, 95, 99, 110, 113
kind, 85
knack, 23, 55
knowledge, 67, 69, 84, 94, 102, 106, 112

label, 7, 26, 28
landscape, 2, 9, 11, 16, 17, 19, 21, 26, 27, 35–37, 41, 49, 54, 57, 58, 75, 76, 79, 82, 84–89, 94, 97, 100–102, 106, 109, 110, 113–115, 118, 119
language, 42, 43
layer, 12, 24, 56, 71, 78, 85
layering, 20, 24, 102, 108
leap, 18
learning, 11, 93, 95, 110, 111
Leeds, 4, 13, 27
legacy, 3, 7, 11, 33, 39, 45–47, 52, 54, 55, 69, 78, 82, 84, 86, 87, 89, 92, 94, 97, 101, 103, 106, 107, 116, 118–120
legend, 7, 52, 54, 92, 97, 107, 114, 116
legwork, 30
lesson, 96, 107
letter, 72
level, 30, 43, 53, 55, 62, 70, 75, 78, 87, 88, 92, 93, 109, 114
liberation, 26
life, 12, 20, 26, 36, 43, 45, 55, 61, 62, 64, 65, 67–70, 72, 80, 92–94, 98, 110
lifeblood, 11, 74
lifestyle, 69, 93, 94

light, 29, 50, 61, 63, 70, 80, 82, 86, 103, 113
lighting, 51, 57, 109
lightning, 11, 49
like, 1, 4–6, 10, 11, 17, 19, 22–24, 27, 30–32, 35–37, 41, 45–48, 58, 63, 67, 69–71, 74, 84, 91, 96, 100, 103, 115, 117
limelight, 30
limit, 20
line, 12
lineage, 9
listener, 24, 110
literature, 101
London, 9, 10, 27, 32, 35, 36
look, 19, 67, 102, 103, 120
loop, 56
looping, 56, 98
loss, 71
love, 2, 10, 11, 13, 40, 66, 67, 69, 74, 81, 91
lover, 5
low, 36
loyalty, 73, 103, 114
lyricism, 105

magic, 11, 23, 30, 45, 54
mainstream, 28, 29, 36, 39, 41, 42, 46, 48, 49, 51, 54, 58, 59, 115, 116
making, 2, 18, 39, 45, 55, 65–67, 78, 85, 98, 110, 115
manipulation, 24
mark, 3–5, 8, 15, 18, 28, 30, 36, 37, 39, 41, 43, 46, 52, 54, 74, 76, 78, 82, 84, 89, 92, 94, 96–98, 101, 106, 107, 113–115, 118, 120

Mark Thompson, 39
market, 42, 65, 95
marketing, 30
mastery, 53, 85, 98
material, 65, 91
matter, 39
meaning, 2, 25
means, 54, 57, 61, 114
mecca, 30
media, 28, 30, 68, 73, 81, 103, 106, 117
meditation, 94
meeting, 39, 65
melody, 11, 13, 47, 48, 84
melting, 9, 14, 32, 44, 71
memoir, 63
memory, 55
mentality, 28, 118
mentor, 43, 102
mentorship, 102, 103, 112
merchandise, 30, 31
message, 22, 73
metal, 100
metropolis, 79
mic, 9, 22
Michael Johnson, 39
Mick Jagger, 104
Middle Eastern, 78
Miles Davis, 11
milestone, 15
mind, 2, 4, 11, 22, 27, 36, 47, 53, 54, 65, 67, 104, 116
mindset, 12, 71, 95
mix, 10, 56, 79, 107
mixing, 53, 114
mold, 82, 84, 93, 108
moment, 11, 26, 42, 44, 45, 50, 52, 53, 67, 70, 72, 99
momentum, 7

moniker, 2, 26
motivation, 66, 67
mouth, 30
movement, 7, 10, 11, 15, 44, 55
multiculturalism, 9, 10
multimedia, 104, 113
mundane, 20, 85
music, 1–33, 36–58, 61–89, 91–120
musicality, 48
musician, 9, 14, 17, 18, 20, 22, 23, 62, 64, 77, 92
musicology, 59
myriad, 99
mystery, 1–3
myth, 3

name, 2, 6, 18, 25–27, 39
narrative, 80
nature, 2, 13, 17, 19, 25, 44, 49, 59, 65, 78, 91, 101
necessity, 84
need, 2, 61, 62, 64, 84, 119
needle, 11
neighborhood, 13
Nero, 37
network, 6, 22, 70
New York City, 42
newfound, 25, 50, 62, 65, 68, 70, 72, 74, 81, 94, 95
niche, 14, 95
nightclub, 27
noise, 19, 48
norm, 119
nostalgia, 32
note, 30, 31, 46, 71
notice, 52, 54
notion, 75, 85
number, 86

obscurity, 6, 107
observer, 5
odyssey, 11, 31
offshoot, 37
on, 2–5, 7, 8, 10–15, 17–19, 22–24, 26–31, 33, 37–43, 45–47, 50–59, 61–76, 78–80, 82–85, 87–89, 91–103, 105–107, 109, 111–120
one, 3, 6, 7, 11, 18, 20, 24, 25, 31, 35, 37, 39, 40, 42, 45–47, 50, 64, 69, 71, 74, 78, 80, 85, 91, 92, 95, 97, 103, 108, 109, 111, 116, 117, 119, 120
online, 22, 28, 30, 46, 102, 106, 117
onslaught, 49
openness, 44
opportunity, 6, 22, 30, 39, 40, 44, 52, 69, 99, 102, 104, 111
orchestra, 30, 75, 104
orchestration, 104
order, 17, 35, 67, 68, 110, 111
oscillator, 36
other, 6, 7, 10–12, 20, 22, 25, 30, 31, 36, 38, 41, 44, 47, 48, 54–56, 58, 66, 69, 72, 78, 80, 82, 84, 96, 97, 106, 110, 114, 119
ounce, 62
outlet, 11, 62
output, 64

pad, 28
pairing, 41, 74
palette, 11, 17, 40, 44, 77, 83, 84, 92, 100, 108, 110
part, 4, 15, 31, 41, 55, 63, 71, 81, 92
partnership, 6, 21, 39, 74–76

party, 27, 64, 98
passion, 4, 6, 9, 12, 13, 21, 22, 25, 26, 28, 31, 39, 41, 43, 52, 54, 55, 62, 66–72, 74, 80, 81, 91, 92, 95, 96, 105, 107, 114, 119
past, 45, 68, 71
path, 2, 4, 8, 11, 12, 15, 16, 29, 33, 36, 45, 61, 62, 64, 67, 68, 70, 72, 80, 82, 84, 91, 93, 96, 101
patter, 12
penchant, 88
people, 19, 30, 43, 102, 105, 110
perception, 54
performance, 30, 33, 36, 42, 43, 51–55, 57, 73, 85, 104, 109, 119
performer, 51, 55
period, 6, 16, 42, 67–69, 72, 80
permission, 117
perseverance, 54, 65, 71, 72, 80, 91, 92, 96, 97, 119
persistence, 96
persona, 37, 103
personality, 99
perspective, 3, 10, 63, 66, 71, 75, 76, 81, 94–96, 115
phase, 39, 111
phenomenon, 36, 54, 92
philanthropic, 119
philosophy, 19
phone, 104
piano, 11
piece, 20, 76
pilgrimage, 2
pinnacle, 52
pioneer, 2, 7, 15, 28, 56, 74, 76, 85–87, 91, 101, 105, 119

pitch, 24, 36
place, 1, 14, 47, 49, 54, 63, 66, 74, 82, 89, 100, 107
platform, 28, 30, 51, 62, 63, 69, 88, 99, 102, 110, 113, 119
play, 41, 56, 63, 112
playground, 75
playlist, 29, 32
point, 14, 15, 33, 62, 65, 67–69, 80
polish, 38
pollination, 40, 78, 88, 98
pool, 22
pop, 36, 37, 41, 51, 58, 100
popularity, 7, 36, 42, 46, 50, 51, 53, 87, 91, 115
population, 10
pore, 55
position, 47, 79, 85–87
pot, 9, 14, 32, 44, 71
potential, 4, 8, 22, 38, 44, 58, 61, 85, 97, 106, 108
power, 4–6, 8, 10, 12, 19, 28, 31, 41, 43, 45, 46, 50, 51, 54, 63, 66, 70, 72, 77, 82, 91–94, 96, 97, 102, 105, 107, 109, 110, 115, 117, 119, 120
precedent, 106
precision, 57
presence, 7, 30, 42, 47, 50, 52–55, 81, 98, 114, 116, 119
pressure, 65, 70
prevalence, 63
principle, 102
privilege, 39, 55
problem, 28, 61
process, 5, 20, 23, 24, 62, 65, 68, 70–73, 76, 80, 82, 100, 109, 112
processing, 24, 38

# Index

prodigy, 12
producer, 15, 18, 20, 21, 23, 27, 40, 41, 47, 58, 75, 112
production, 14, 17, 18, 22, 25, 29, 36–38, 40, 45–47, 57, 73, 77, 79, 85, 87, 89, 98, 100, 102, 106–108, 110, 112–114
professional, 61, 64–67, 70, 72, 79, 80, 95
profile, 105
program, 62, 64, 67
project, 51, 101, 104, 112
proliferation, 58
prominence, 58
prowess, 17, 38, 47, 75
psyche, 4
pulsating, 2, 9, 20, 27, 36, 38, 46, 57, 73, 105
pulse, 4, 30
punk, 2, 9, 21, 44
purpose, 68–70, 74
pursuit, 3, 5, 6, 8, 12, 14, 15, 22, 23, 39, 52, 57, 63, 71, 85, 87, 96, 101, 107, 109, 111, 119, 120

quake, 54
quality, 38, 48, 62, 75, 101
quest, 2, 11, 18, 24–26, 30, 56, 75, 83, 92, 107, 108
quo, 5, 17–19, 26, 45, 50, 78, 92, 96, 98, 106, 113, 116, 117, 120

radio, 37, 41, 42
rain, 20
range, 4, 5, 9, 13, 15, 18, 21, 32, 38, 44, 47, 53, 65, 72, 73, 75, 78, 83, 84, 91, 96, 99, 101

rap, 21, 58
rapper, 40, 47, 75, 105
rave, 4
reach, 8, 22, 30, 37, 41, 49, 81, 113
reader, 36, 37
realism, 24, 85
reality, 3, 61, 67, 110
realization, 66, 94, 95
realm, 4, 12, 22, 28, 37, 58, 75, 84, 87, 105, 107, 108, 118
rebel, 1, 5, 11, 12, 18, 25, 26, 29, 45, 56, 74, 91, 92, 99, 101, 119, 120
rebellion, 26, 27
rebirth, 26
rebuilding, 64, 68, 80, 82
recipe, 46
recognition, 8, 42, 44, 74, 102
record, 7, 10, 11, 28, 33
recorder, 79
recording, 12
recovery, 16, 61–65, 67–70, 80–82, 92, 93, 119
redemption, 63, 68, 73, 81, 92
rediscovery, 70, 71
reflection, 5, 23, 46, 62, 66, 68, 70, 71, 82, 93–95
refusal, 15, 98
reggae, 3, 9, 10, 13, 14, 16–18, 21, 23, 31, 32, 37, 38, 44, 47, 48, 53, 75, 77, 83, 85, 87, 91, 97, 99, 100, 102, 106, 113, 115, 119
region, 33
rehab, 65, 68–70, 80
rehabilitation, 62, 64, 65, 67, 70, 80, 93
reinvention, 39, 74, 92, 105
rejuvenation, 67

relatability, 68, 85
relationship, 30, 31, 59, 69
release, 14, 39, 47, 62
relevance, 43, 76
reminder, 18, 45, 63, 69, 74, 82, 92, 97, 98, 116, 119, 120
remix, 58, 75
remixing, 51
renewal, 82
repertoire, 19, 49
representation, 26
reputation, 7, 27, 29, 32, 42, 52, 53, 74
resilience, 14–16, 39, 49, 50, 62–65, 68–70, 73, 74, 80–82, 93, 95, 96, 119, 120
resistance, 29, 85
resolve, 28
resonance, 58
respect, 22
response, 14
rest, 57, 111
result, 20, 23, 36, 38, 53, 74, 84, 100, 104, 111
resurgence, 37, 81
return, 72, 74
revenue, 113
revolution, 10, 26, 36, 37, 45, 76
rhythm, 13, 19, 23, 84
ride, 12, 37
right, 9
Rihanna, 58
rise, 1, 6, 7, 11, 12, 18, 26–28, 36, 37, 42, 46, 48, 52, 53, 58, 61, 64, 67, 74, 82, 87, 91, 93
risk, 49
road, 67
rock, 9, 11, 21, 28, 36, 44, 82, 88, 104, 117
rod, 49
role, 1, 6, 9, 10, 22, 23, 32, 36, 47, 54, 58, 63, 81, 89, 91, 92, 97, 99, 100, 102, 106, 108, 112, 115, 118
room, 55
roster, 28
rush, 59
Rusko, 1–32, 37–57, 61–89, 91–120
rut, 65

safety, 29
sailing, 61
sake, 48
sample, 33, 78
sampling, 17, 20, 23, 24, 38, 51, 85, 112
San Francisco, 42
sanctuary, 1
sauce, 74
scenario, 79
scene, 1, 3–6, 9, 10, 13, 18, 19, 21, 25, 26, 28, 32, 33, 35, 37, 39, 41, 42, 44, 46, 47, 51, 52, 54, 57, 58, 73, 74, 84, 89, 91, 97, 99, 100, 102, 103, 106, 118
schedule, 65
sci, 59
screen, 58
search, 2, 25, 26, 107
secret, 2, 74
section, 6, 12, 17, 18, 21, 25, 26, 43, 46, 50, 52, 58, 61, 74, 76, 82, 84, 87, 92, 99, 101, 106, 107, 111, 113, 116

Index 137

Selah Sue, 114
self, 3, 15, 16, 26, 62, 63, 66–72, 80, 82, 93–96
sensation, 36, 47
sense, 10, 12, 24, 30, 32, 51, 58, 68, 69, 73, 74, 81, 88, 103, 119
series, 14, 23, 26, 27, 32, 42, 64, 65, 95, 112
serve, 5, 75, 92, 116, 120
set, 6, 7, 13, 15, 20, 25, 28, 29, 37, 38, 43, 44, 47, 51–55, 57, 65, 91, 96, 98, 100, 101, 106, 111, 113, 114, 119
setback, 16
setting, 12, 26, 53, 85, 95, 98, 106, 116
setup, 57
severity, 62
shadow, 48
shape, 2, 10, 11, 14, 19, 37, 39, 45, 52, 69, 85, 89, 94, 97, 101, 103, 107, 113, 116
share, 7, 15, 22, 30, 67, 81, 91, 103
sheet, 11
shift, 54, 58
shore, 101
show, 22, 50, 55, 105, 119
showcase, 6, 28, 52, 99
side, 64, 69, 80, 93
sight, 66
sign, 48
signature, 2, 14, 17, 32, 38, 40, 43, 47–50, 53, 56, 65, 73, 75, 88, 97, 104, 111, 114, 115
significance, 63, 95
silver, 58
Simon Reynolds, 29
singer, 41, 75
single, 17, 21, 31, 44, 47, 77, 82, 88

skepticism, 15, 57, 104
skill, 47, 96
Skream, 22, 36
smile, 53
smoke, 55
sobriety, 62
society, 63
socio, 59
software, 12, 18, 20, 77, 100, 108
solace, 6, 61, 64, 67
solo, 31, 32, 38
song, 19, 23, 41, 50, 76
songwriter, 41, 75
soul, 2, 9, 11, 17, 105
sound, 2–8, 10–12, 14, 17, 18, 20–32, 36–41, 43, 44, 46–49, 51–59, 65, 66, 70, 72–75, 77–79, 81–85, 87, 88, 92, 94, 95, 97, 99–104, 106–109, 111–120
soundscape, 59
soundtrack, 37, 58
source, 9, 13, 23, 26, 28, 61, 82, 97, 102
South London, 37, 44
space, 38, 56, 58
spark, 65, 66, 70, 81
speaker, 36
spectacle, 53, 55, 57, 114
spectator, 55
sphere, 58, 88, 97, 109
spin, 39
spirit, 2, 4, 5, 9, 16, 25, 28, 41, 50, 63, 76, 89, 91, 103, 109, 120
sponge, 4
spontaneity, 51, 57, 85
spot, 52, 56

spotlight, 6, 15, 26, 41, 50, 66, 67, 72–74, 115
stage, 7, 12, 25, 26, 30, 37, 42, 46, 50, 52–55, 57, 58, 73, 98, 105, 114, 116, 119
stance, 48
standard, 19, 51, 57, 98, 100, 114
standout, 47
star, 27, 32, 105
stardom, 6, 28, 30, 36, 41, 48, 64, 67, 107
start, 19, 22, 72
starting, 33, 42
state, 105
statement, 105
status, 5, 6, 17–19, 26, 42, 45, 50, 52–54, 78, 87, 92, 96, 98, 99, 101, 105, 106, 113, 116, 117, 120
steampunk, 59
step, 28, 30, 35, 40, 65–67, 72, 78, 92, 93, 109, 114
Stephen Thomas Erlewine, 29
stone, 14
storm, 49
story, 3, 8, 12, 39, 50, 57, 63, 68, 69, 71, 73, 74, 82, 92, 96, 98
storytelling, 17
strategy, 81
streaming, 47
street, 10, 19, 20, 23, 79
strength, 16, 65, 67, 93
stretching, 24
structure, 84
student, 59
studio, 20, 27, 47
study, 11
stuff, 7

style, 11, 13, 17, 22, 29–31, 44, 45, 49, 59, 77, 87, 88, 99, 107, 111, 115, 116
sub, 108, 116
subculture, 36, 54
subgenre, 100
substance, 16, 61–65, 67, 68, 70, 72, 80, 92, 93, 119
subwoofer, 36
success, 8, 12, 15, 16, 28, 30, 32, 42, 43, 46–53, 59, 63, 66, 67, 80, 88, 93, 95, 96, 98, 101, 103, 104, 107, 113, 116–118
SuChin Pak, 114
summer, 13
superstar, 43
support, 7, 31, 32, 62–66, 68, 69, 80, 95, 103
surprise, 23, 104
surrounding, 66, 69, 96, 111
suspense, 58
sustainability, 113
swagger, 17
symbol, 26, 49
symphony, 30
synchrony, 4
synergy, 21, 41, 58
synthesis, 24, 109
synthesizer, 85
synthetic, 51, 85
system, 80

table, 19, 20, 22, 96, 110
take, 2, 11, 17–19, 22, 31, 33, 45, 51, 52, 54, 58, 67, 70, 71, 78, 96, 98, 102, 105, 107, 111, 116, 117
taker, 49

tale, 63
talent, 1, 3, 6, 9, 13, 14, 43, 49, 52–55, 61, 72, 76, 86, 92, 102, 106, 111
tapestry, 1, 3, 5, 9, 10, 18, 22, 23, 32, 44, 70, 79, 110
task, 43, 62
taste, 3, 29
team, 53
technique, 85, 109
techno, 84
technology, 53, 56, 57, 77, 101, 108–110, 112
television, 42
tempos, 44
tender, 13
term, 95
territory, 43, 76, 117
test, 64
testament, 7, 16, 20, 23, 43, 45, 46, 49, 50, 53–55, 63, 70, 74, 80, 81, 87, 91, 92, 94, 101, 109, 114, 119
testimony, 96
texture, 20, 24, 32, 85
the Balkan Mountains, 25
the United States, 42
therapy, 62, 65, 68, 70, 80, 93
thing, 3, 116
thought, 20, 105, 108, 110
thread, 26
time, 5, 11–13, 21, 24, 30, 31, 37, 38, 40, 46, 49, 53, 55, 56, 67, 68, 71, 74, 76, 80, 85, 95, 110, 120
today, 12, 19, 25, 100, 115
Tokyo, 43
toll, 61, 64, 65, 67, 70, 80, 91
tool, 110

top, 46, 47, 115
topping, 7, 40, 47, 50, 58, 75
touch, 30, 31, 33, 119
tour, 43
touring, 42, 61, 64, 65
town, 91
track, 5, 15, 20, 23, 33, 38, 40–42, 46, 47, 75, 83, 84, 104, 105
traction, 59
tradition, 117
traffic, 79
trailblazer, 78, 102
trailblazing, 10, 101, 116
trajectory, 3, 5, 9, 15
transformation, 2, 5, 25, 68, 81, 92, 94
transition, 37, 52
transparency, 68
transport, 48, 109
trap, 73, 88, 116
trapstep, 58
treatment, 64, 65
trial, 94
trip, 25
triumph, 16
trumpet, 11
trust, 31, 68, 79–82
truth, 2
turmoil, 62
turn, 48
turning, 14, 15, 24, 42, 48, 62, 65, 67–69, 80
turntable, 11
twist, 51, 79, 104

UK, 4, 6, 35, 39–41, 47, 58
underground, 2–4, 6, 9, 10, 13, 27, 29, 36, 37, 39, 41, 43, 44, 49, 51, 54, 55, 58, 115

understanding, 9, 46, 63, 66, 68, 78, 81, 84, 87
unfamiliar, 18, 71
union, 10
uniqueness, 50, 66
United Kingdom, 27
unity, 55, 119
universe, 3, 5, 10, 55
unpredictability, 78
up, 4, 9–11, 13, 18, 21, 28, 32, 41, 44, 47, 48, 50, 52, 56, 57, 65, 66, 84, 96, 97, 99, 104, 108, 111, 114
upbringing, 5, 10, 44
urge, 95
urgency, 58
use, 23, 24, 32, 33, 49, 51, 56, 57, 63, 77, 85, 98, 108–110, 113, 114

value, 30, 38, 44, 96
variant, 100
variety, 4, 44, 77, 111, 117
Vegas, 75
vehicle, 110
venture, 18, 38, 43, 76, 100, 108, 109
venue, 55
versatility, 41, 47, 72, 75, 83
verse, 19
version, 93
vibe, 58
vibrancy, 49
video, 57–59, 98
village, 25
vinyl, 11, 12, 99
vision, 7, 10, 19, 23, 25, 26, 28, 29, 32, 45, 50, 65, 92, 95, 99, 100, 107, 110, 111, 113, 118, 120

visionary, 4, 87, 109
visual, 20, 29, 50, 51, 53, 55, 57, 59, 66, 101, 104, 109, 110, 112, 113
Vladimir Bogdanov, 29
vocal, 24, 44, 46, 79
voice, 3, 6, 14, 32, 66, 72, 74, 95
volume, 48
vortex, 55
vulnerability, 63, 67, 93, 94

wake, 88
warehouse, 2, 27, 36
wave, 19, 26, 27, 38, 43, 49, 66, 97, 106, 116, 117
way, 14, 19–23, 26, 35, 37, 42, 48, 52, 54, 66, 69, 72, 76, 82, 88, 93, 97, 101, 106, 112, 115–117
wealth, 10, 102
web, 5
website, 24, 30
well, 30, 31, 59, 61, 64, 67–70, 76, 79, 80, 82, 91, 92, 94, 95, 107
while, 2, 11, 25, 28, 32, 49, 56, 66, 73, 75, 87, 88, 95, 100
whole, 18, 41, 51, 52, 89, 109
wildfire, 41
willingness, 17–19, 28, 33, 40, 41, 43, 44, 76, 78, 82, 84, 88, 89, 92, 93, 100, 101, 105–108, 114, 116, 117, 119
wind, 1
windowpane, 12
wisdom, 2, 94, 96, 97
wizardry, 46
wobble, 36

wonder, 1, 105
word, 31, 50
work, 6, 7, 22, 30, 38, 40, 48, 52, 53, 57, 64, 71, 72, 74, 81, 88, 89, 92, 95, 96, 102, 103, 107, 110, 114, 116
world, 3–5, 7, 12, 14, 15, 18, 21–25, 32, 36, 37, 40, 41, 43, 45–47, 49, 50, 52, 54, 56, 57, 75–78, 84–87, 91, 92, 96–98, 101, 104, 105, 107, 110, 113, 114, 118–120

writing, 66

yourself, 28, 45

Zed Bias, 35
Zeds Dead, 102
zone, 18, 40, 78, 92, 96, 109

Milton Keynes UK
Ingram Content Group UK Ltd.
UKHW020750051024
449151UK00011B/498